HOW TO MAKE
WINES AT HOME

HOW TO MAKE WINES AT HOME

Kenneth Hawkins

ROBINSON

First published in Great Britain in 1986 by Elliot Right Way
This paperback edition published in 2014 by Robinson

Copyright © Elliot Right Way, 1986, 2014

The moral right of the author has been asserted.

All rights reserved.
No part of this publication may be reproduced, stored in a retrieval system, or
transmitted, in any form, or by any means, without the prior permission in
writing of the publisher, nor be otherwise circulated in any form of binding or
cover other than that in which it is published and without a similar condition
including this condition being imposed on the subsequent purchaser.

A CIP catalogue record for this book
is available from the British Library.

ISBN 978-0-71602-382-1 (paperback)
ISBN 978-0-71602-383-8 (ebook)

Typeset in Adobe Garamond by Basement Press, Glaisdale
Printed and bound by CPI Group (UK) Ltd, Croydon, CR0 4YY

Robinson
is an imprint of
Constable & Robinson Ltd
100 Victoria Embankment
London EC4Y 0DY

An Hachette UK Company
www.hachette.co.uk

www.constablerobinson.com

CONTENTS

1
INTRODUCTION

Noah was the first man to plant the vine
'He drank of the wine and was drunk' – Genesis
– the story goes that he lived to the age of 350 years.

There was a time in my life when I did not make wine – it was a long while ago, but I can still remember it vaguely. Before I was married, my father 'dabbled' in the hobby, but neither his efforts, nor the results, interested me greatly, and although I have always been fond of good living, circumstances at that time only allowed for the tasting of a commercial wine on very rare occasions. My attitude to country wines was rather condescending – it was a substitute, and I was a perfectionist. In any case, the hobby was not active enough for someone who was fond of almost any form of physical exercise. However, time goes by, as it is apt to do, and this, together with a rather serious illness, left me without a hobby, and feeling very sorry for myself.

To the clergyman who introduced me to winemaking, I shall be forever indebted, for he did much more than give me an absorbing hobby. He gave me a renewed interest in life at a time when it was really needed, and apart from that hobby, the introduction to a host of new friends through a winemaking club, and a comradeship there that I have rarely found elsewhere. (See Chapter 11 for the advantages to be gained from belonging to a winemaking club).

As a result of my experience, my main concern has always been to try to help the beginner and in doing so to *keep it simple*. This is for two reasons: firstly as our hobby can be simple if that is what we want of it; and secondly, due to the fact that I am no chemist anyway. I may comment on many of the modern sophisticated items now available to us, but my strong advice to those about to take up this fascinating hobby is, do not initially buy a lot of expensive equipment – learn your craft first, let your enthusiasm build up, and gradually add those little extras as you feel the need for them.

Though I hope to cover most aspects of the craft during the course of the book, the 'Purists' may well be disappointed, for it will contain my personal experiences, some of which may not follow the accepted pattern. I do not apologise for this, since my results have brought a fair amount of success over the past few years, and in any case, I have found so many conflicting statements in some of the books that are now available, that I am sure that I am not alone in writing from my own experience.

Although this book is not intended to be a textbook for the experienced winemaker, I feel that many of the recipes, and their layout, may be of interest to all those who enjoy participation in the craft.

Winemaking has probably become one of the most popular craft hobbies and has many attractions for those who appreciate the odd glass of wine, either with a meal, or simply on a social occasion. In these days of high taxation, our own wines are relatively cheap to make, and the hobby gives a feeling of achievement in the same way as the ability to cook an excellent meal. But unlike cooking, it is a hobby that can occupy the individual for two hours a month or twenty, according to the time and space available, and the degree of enthusiasm that the hobby has created. (Before we go any further, it must be pointed out that the law in Great Britain allows us to make any amount of wine for *our own consumption*, but we must not sell a drop, or allow it to be sold for profit, as no duty has been paid. Neither are we allowed to distil).

The declared definition of wine is an alcoholic beverage made from the fermented juice of the grape, fermented in the country of origin – all of which may be quite acceptable to the countries whose climates permit the growing of grapes in sufficient quantities to enable them to fulfil their needs, and possibly to export, but it is hardly satisfactory for countries such as the U.K. Nowadays the utilisation of other fruits etc. has become such an interesting craft that there are thousands of 'amateurs' (and I use this word with trepidation, for many of them know a great deal both about the ingredients used, and the commercial wines of the world) who are quite capable of making an alcoholic drink which is at least the equal of the middle range commercial product. Of course there are many whose efforts leave much to be desired – producing alcoholic drinks, perhaps, but for one reason or another, not up to the standard.

I hope that this book will enable anyone, even those who are new to the craft, to reach an acceptable level. By this I do not mean that all wines should become copies of the commercial product, but simply that we use them as a comparison for quality, as obviously a commercial wine must have a market value, and this becomes the best standard the amateur winemaker has to set against his or her own efforts.

As you will see, our home-made wines can be produced from an infinite variety of ingredients – flowers, fruit, grain, honey, leaves and vegetables – but experience will probably show that the best results will usually be obtained from a recipe that includes an element of fruit in it, otherwise there may be a tendency for a lack of vinosity in the finished wine. By all means experiment with other available ingredients later on, but it is better for the beginner to learn his or her craft first, before going into the intricacies of blending ingredients without the aid of a proven recipe.

Home-made wines have been made in this country for hundreds of years, using fruits from the hedgerows, flowers, vegetables etc., with honey as the sweetening agent. The first set-back to home winemaking came when the Bordeaux area fell under British rule, and for many years imports of French wines were enjoyed by the more prosperous, leaving the making of country wines to the poorer classes. Later, when those territories were lost, wines were imported from Portugal, with whom Britain had a trade treaty. In the eighteenth century the quantity of sugar imported caused the price to fall within reach of the working man, and from then onwards the use of honey declined, and gradually malt beers began to take over. As a nation, the making of wines declined, and it was indeed fortunate for us that our forebears kept, and handed down, many of the old recipes, for they are still the basis of some of our country wines today.

Many of us have heard stories of how strong the home-made wines were 'in Grandma's day'. Don't believe a word of it. Present-day yeast strains and expertise are infinitely superior. It was simply that in those days the cheapness of spirits made it possible for home-made wines to be fortified with brandy. Those days are gone, and if our wines are to be as strong, we must bring this about by our own efforts, such as the control of sugar, and the use of the appropriate yeast culture, in order to keep down costs.

These last forty years have seen significant advances in the craft. New strains of yeast have become available, fining and filtering methods have been greatly improved, and with these better facilities, and the knowledge of how the alcoholic content can be controlled, we are now able to produce what we know as 'Purpose Wines', i.e. aperitifs, table wines, dessert wines, sparkling wines, and even liqueurs (or wines for before, during and after the meal) and I will go into these in detail in Chapter 5.

Finally, never be afraid to ask advice from an experienced winemaker – I have always found them to be most helpful.

THE ORIGINS OF WINEMAKING

Before going on to the equipment which will be needed, I would like to include a little story of the very early days of winemaking;

interesting, although I cannot guarantee its accuracy. However, I would not quarrel with the description of the wine, for taken in moderation, wine can be an aid to the digestion, is full of vitamins, and in fact is one of God's great gifts to mankind.

Jamshed, first king of the Persians, and according to legend a grandson of Noah, became an old man and lost his teeth, but he so liked the grape that he ordered his servants to press a large quantity so that he could enjoy the juice. As he wished to have the juice throughout the winter months, the stock was to be kept in great containers. After a few days, however, he noticed that the juice had changed its appearance and tasted bitter. He was very sad, and thought that the juice had gone bad and was poisonous. In order that no one should inadvertently drink it, he ordered that it should be placed in the cellar, the door locked, and on the cellar door, the word 'Poisonous' printed.

Soon afterwards a favourite slave had a terrible headache which caused her many sleepless nights, and she felt that she wanted to die. Finally she thought of the poisonous juice, and crept down to the cellar. After sampling the juice, she began to feel quite happy and could no longer feel the pain. The more she drank, the better she felt, until she finally fell asleep in the cellar. In the meantime her absence had been noticed, and a search for her began. After a while she was found, but she continued to sleep for two days and two nights – it is said mainly from the exhaustion of those sleepless nights. She finally woke to find the king present and very anxious about her. The headache was gone and she felt in the best of health. The king was so overjoyed that he, too, decided to sample the 'poison'. He also became happy and carefree, and gave the drink the name of the 'Medicine of Kings'.

2
EQUIPMENT

What do we need in the way of equipment? At the outset, keep it simple. Don't buy a lot of sophisticated equipment until you are sure that you really need it. The following is a list of what is either essential, or at least advisable.

- A two-gallon (nine-litre) bucket, preferably of good quality, rigid, white, non-toxic plastic. (Avoid the use of earthenware, which may be lead-based; enamel, which if crazed may taint a wine by contact with metal; and also any brass or copper containers).
- A cover for the bucket, either a plastic lid, or a sheet of plastic which can be tied on to exclude air.
- A large sieve or piece of muslin.
- A large funnel, preferably large enough for the sieve to fit into it.
- A large wooden or plastic spoon.
- Glass jars or demijohns – the quantity will depend on the individual, but always keep one empty jar for use in syphoning off the wine.
- Non-toxic plastic containers may be used for short-term purposes, but not for storage, and do not use a plastic container which has previously been used for vinegar.
- Airlocks, airlock bungs and either corks or rubber bungs for each jar – I prefer the rubber ones as they are easier to sterilise.
- A length of rubber or plastic tubing for syphoning off the wine.
- A hydrometer and jar (more about this in Chapter 7).
- A corker for use when bottling.
- A supply of citric acid, tartaric acid and straight corks.
- A quantity of bottles, preferably punted (i.e. not flat-based).

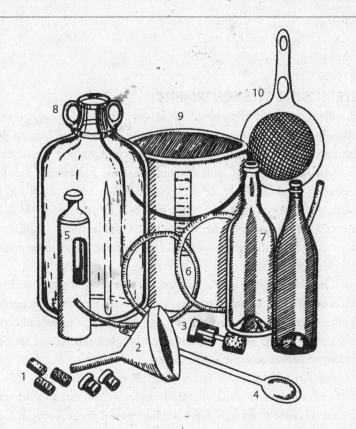

FIG. 1
SOME EQUIPMENT
1. Corks (straight and competition-type)
2. Plastic funnel
3. Airlock and cork
4. Large plastic or wooden spoon
5. A corker or 'flogger'
6. Rubber or plastic syphon tube
7. Punted bottles for red and white wines
8. Glass demijohn or fermentation jar
9. Two-gallon (nine-litre) plastic bucket
10. Sieve

- Labels.
- A bottle brush.
- A thermometer.

STERILISING THE EQUIPMENT

It will be noticed that there is no mention of any agent for sterilising the equipment in the above list. Cleanliness is possibly the most important aspect of winemaking, and yet one which can so easily be overlooked. It is not only that the equipment should appear to be clean, it should be *chemically* clean. Hot water and a brush are all very well, but a quick swill will not necessarily kill all bacteria. The use of either Campden tablets or a sodium metabisulphite solution is essential if the ingredients are to be given the best possible start.

If Campden tablets are to be used, dissolve two, together with a saltspoonful of citric acid, in one pint (½ litre) of water, and thoroughly cleanse all equipment to be used. If made in larger quantities and kept in a tightly corked jar, this solution may be used and re-used over a prolonged period before it begins to lose its efficiency.

Campden tablets are in fact sodium metabisulphite, and whilst they are convenient to handle, and obviously the quantity of the chemical is easy to assess when in tablet form, it is cheaper to make up a sterilising solution using sodium metabisulphite in powder form: 5 oz (140g) to the gallon (4.5 litres) or ½ oz (14g) to the pint (½ litre). One word of warning: do *not* breathe the sulphur dioxide fumes given off when the sodium metabisulphate or Campden tablets are mixed with water.

Having prepared the solution, place some in jars, bottles and funnel, using a stiff brush to assist in cleaning off. The airlocks and syphoning tube should also be soaked for a few minutes. Perhaps the most important of all is the plastic bucket into which the must will be placed. Inevitably these buckets become scratched in time, and thereby provide an ideal hiding place for bacteria. Leave the solution in the bucket for a few minutes, and then rinse it out with hot water before use. Once the bucket is as germ-free as possible, care must be taken to ensure that bacteria is not re-introduced by the ingredients themselves – to be entirely free is very difficult, but wash the fruit, particularly dried fruit which is coated with a preservative when packed. When the ingredients and water are all in the bucket, add one Campden tablet and leave overnight. After 24 hours the yeast starter may be added, and should soon provide the protection of alcohol which will kill off any remaining bacteria cells before any lasting damage can be done.

Beware of friends who insist that they never use more than hot water – they may appear to be safe for some considerable time, but there could be a day of reckoning, and down the drain goes a gallon of wine and a lot of effort.

Having given a list of equipment needed, perhaps I should explain a few of the terms that are found in winemaking.

AIRLOCK OR FERMENTATION LOCK

There are many types, in glass or in plastic, and although some types look complicated and highly professional, the simplest little plastic airlock is quite adequate. As the name suggests, the airlock protects the fermenting ingredients by excluding the air, which could cause oxidation, and gives protection from the vinegar or fruit fly, which is one of our greatest enemies, whilst still allowing the carbon dioxide gas to escape into the atmosphere. The airlock should always be kept half-filled with water.

BODY

The fullness of a wine – the best illustration is the comparison between a light table wine and a heavy port. Table wines are generally light- to medium-bodied, whereas ports and dessert wines are full-bodied.

CAP
This is the fermenting head of the liquor which contains quantities of the ingredients raised to the surface by the action of the yeast.

CARBON DIOXIDE
A colourless, odourless gas, produced by the yeast during the fermentation process, which must be allowed to escape into the atmosphere. If retained in the jar or bottle, the gas will build up pressure which will ultimately burst the container. Carbon dioxide is heavier than air, and will therefore form a protective blanket over the fermenting must in the early stages.

DRY
A term given to a wine from which the sugar has fermented out completely.

ENZYMES
These are organic catalysts produced by the living yeast cells. There are many different types in our wines, each having one specific job to do. It should be remembered that as wine is a living thing, changes will be taking place throughout its life.

FERMENTATION ON THE PULP
The first heavy or aerobic fermentation (see page 15).

FILTERING
A method of extracting particles of solids and dead yeast cells from a wine which has not cleared naturally. Filtering should be used as a last resort, for it does, on occasions, affect the flavour of a wine, particularly if it is a light, delicate, table wine.

FINING
Preferable to filtering, but even so, do let Nature try to clear a wine first. There are several types of fining agents, and sachets are often issued with many of the kits now on the market – this is simply to

allow the beginner to produce a drinkable wine at an earlier date, but with a little patience any well-balanced wine should clear by itself, and the slightly longer wait will be amply repaid by the production of a better and more matured wine. I shall be going further into this in later chapters.

GRAVITY (S.G.)
Short for specific gravity, the measurement used to check the degree of sweetness of a wine. If taken at the beginning of the ferment with the hydrometer, and again at the end, a calculation can be made which will give the alcoholic content of the finished wine. The method will be shown later when we consider the use of the hydrometer in Chapter 7.

LEES
The yeast and solid deposit formed during fermentation.

LIQUOR
The liquid containing sugar and other ingredients which will eventually become wine when the yeast has completed its work.

MUST
The pulp or basic ingredients from which the wine is made.

NUTRIENT OR NUTRIENT SALTS
A yeast food.

OXIDATION
The effect caused in a wine by too much contact with the air. Though acceptable in a sherry wine, it is objectionable in a light table wine. The only possible cure for this is to make a further batch of the same wine, and when it is in full ferment, add the oxidised wine, and continue the ferment in the usual way. It is essential that the quantity of oxidised wine added does not exceed the second batch in volume, and I would not even advise this cure if the original wine was badly oxidised.

PURPOSE WINES

Wines that are made for the occasion of a meal. These consist of aperitifs (for before the meal), table wines (drunk during the meal) and dessert wines (sweeter, heavier wines which are consumed after the meal). This, of course, means we must learn to control the alcoholic content far more accurately, and this again brings us into contact with the hydrometer, a most useful instrument in winemaking, which I will go into fully in Chapter 7.

RACKING

Syphoning off the wine from the lees.

STABLE

The condition of the wine when all fermentation has ceased, i.e. when all the yeast cells have been inhibited by the alcohol produced.

SULPHITING THE MUST

Adding a crushed or soluble Campden tablet the day before the yeast is added, ensuring freedom from bacteria.

SECOND RUN

Using the basic materials for a second time in order to produce a lighter table wine. It is usually necessary to add acid and either raisins or sultanas in order to ensure vinosity, and if undertaken, I would suggest a short fermentation on the pulp.

STARTER BOTTLE

Using a starter bottle is the best method of starting a fermentation. A starter is usually prepared at least 24 hours before preparation of the must, or 48 hours if using a liquid yeast.

Ingredients
340ml (12 fl oz) water
3 tsp sugar

¼ tsp citric acid
Juice of an orange
Sachet of a suitable wine yeast or tsp of general purpose wine yeast
Pinch of nutrient salts

Method

Boil the water and then allow it to cool to about 75°F (24°C). Place it in a small bottle, add the sugar, citric acid and the juice of the orange. Mix in the wine yeast and add the nutrient salts. Plug the bottle with cotton wool, and keep the starter in a warm place. When the starter is well under way, stir it into the must.

VINOSITY
This is a term used to identify the wine-like nature of an alcoholic drink.

3
FERMENTATION

Fermentation is in reality a complete series of processes, and is controlled by enzymes which are produced by the yeast cells themselves. Simplified, and as far as we are concerned, it is a process by which the yeast breaks down sugar into its constituent parts of glucose and fructose and gradually converts them into alcohol and carbon dioxide in almost equal proportions, together with several smaller biproducts, of which glycerol (2%) and succinic acid (1% of the alcoholic content) are the most important. (Glycerol adds body to a wine, and succinic acid assists to promote ester production, which in turn, gives the vinous character we need).

A sound fermentation of the must is of great importance to us, and it should begin as soon as possible after the ingredients are in the bucket and the effect of the Campden tablet has worn off. It is for this reason that I would always advocate the use of a starter bottle (see page 12), as it minimises the 'time-lag' when the must is most vulnerable to the growth of bacteria; for in creating the ideal temperature for the yeast to work, we have also produced the best conditions for the growth of bacteria.

To do its work, the yeast must have the right environment – that is, a temperature of 65–75°F (18–24°C) in a sweetened liquid with some acidity. The starter will quickly produce a blanket of carbon dioxide over the fermenting must, and this will help to protect it from bacteria as long as the bucket is covered. The must should be stirred at least once a day, firstly to break up the 'cap' of solids forced to the surface by the yeast, secondly to obtain the best possible extraction, and thirdly in order to introduce a little oxygen into the must. For the best results, an even temperature of about 21°C (70°F) should be maintained throughout the fermentation.

The first heavy ferment is known as the 'aerobic' ferment (or open to some air), and this will continue for four or five days. As soon as it subsides, the must should be strained by using a sieve or piece of muslin, and the liquor placed in a demijohn under airlock, making sure that the jar is topped up to within 1½ in (38mm) of the cork with water. The fermentation will then continue more slowly in what is known as the 'anaerobic' fermentation.

The speed of a complete ferment will vary considerably from one wine to another, and it is not always the fastest fermenting yeast that provides the best wine. An early start and a steady ferment are the keys. A ferment will proceed until the yeast has either used up all the sugar, in which case it is a dry wine, or alternatively, until the amount of alcohol produced has inhibited the yeast cells, which have died, leaving a sweet wine. This, then, gives us a most important piece of knowledge – the amount of sugar controls the dryness of the finished wine, remembering, of course, that some fruits have a greater amount of natural sugar than others, and this natural sugar must be taken into account when assessing the requirements for any particular wine.

You will know the fermentation is complete when the bubbles stop bubbling through the airlock into the outside air, but make sure that fermentation has not stopped for some other reason (see page 51 on stuck ferments). Those using a hydrometer should refer to page 40 for the recognised finishing gravities.

4
BALANCE

In order to obtain the best possible fermentation, it is essential that the balance of ingredients is right. The grape is the only fruit to have this balance, which is acid, flavour, sugar, tannin, water and yeast. Therefore our recipes must contain all these ingredients as nearly as possible in the same proportion if we are to produce a quality wine (see Charts 1 and 2). As none of our fruits is complete in itself, it is not unusual for more than one to be blended in order to obtain this balance. Another way to achieve the right balance is to add grape concentrate, but I suggest only a small quantity. This also improves the vinosity of the wine.

ACID

Because many of our fruits and other winemaking ingredients are short of acid to a greater or lesser degree, some addition will probably be necessary. This acid may be added in several ways – it may be by means of a lemon, or grapes, or just a dry acid. I believe that the dry acid method is best, for it is the only simple way to control the *quantity*.

After all, if the recipe calls for the addition of one lemon, is it a large one? Small one? Extra dry? Or extra juicy? No one knows how much acid has really been added, and even if the result gives a perfect balance, there is very little chance of repeating it.

The acid found in the lemon is citric, and this is probably the most widely used. However, it is not the only acid to be found in the ingredients suitable for winemaking. Tartaric acid is found in grapes; malic acid in apples and most of the stone fruits, and also

CHART 1
TABLE FOR SELECTING INGREDIENTS
FOR BALANCED RED WINES

Using the chart below you can compare the amounts of aroma, acid, tannin and flavour contained in different fruits etc. with the ideal amounts contained in black grapes.

FRUIT	AROMA	ACID	TANNIN	FLAVOUR
Black Grapes*	**XX**	**XXX**	**XXX**	**XX**
Blackberries (fresh)	XX	X	XX	XXXX
Blackberries	XXX	XXXX	XX	XXXX
Blackcurrants	X	XXX	XX	X to XX
Black Plums	XX	XX	X	XX
Cherries (eating)	XX	XX	X	XX
Cherries (morello)	XXX	XXX	X	XXXX
Damsons	XX	XXXX	X	XXX
Elderberries	X	X	XXXX	XX
Loganberries	XXXX	XXX	X	XXX
Mulberries	X	XXX	XX	XX
Raspberries	XXXX	XX	X	XXX
Redcurrants	XX	XXX	X	X
Red Grape Concentrate	X to XX	XX	X to XX	X
Sloes	XX	XXX	XXXX	XXX
Strawberries	XX	X	X	X to XX

* 100% juice; others: 1.8kg (4 lb) per gallon.

17

to a lesser degree in grapes. It follows that all these acids may also be used in powder form, and indeed, I believe that a mixture of all three will produce the best results. 50% tartaric, 30% malic, and 20% citric would seem to be an excellent blend, bearing in mind the acid content of the fruits we are using. Chart 3 shows the different types of acid found in fruits and flowers etc. (Remember, however, that where a fruit is shown to have more than one acid, the number of parts shown on the chart is only a ratio, and does not mean that because a fruit has ten parts it is more acid than one with less parts – an example of this is the strawberry, which although low in acid has a nine to one proportion of citric to malic).

TANNIN

When we come to tannin, we find that some of our ingredients are so bland that its addition may also be advisable (see Charts 1 and 2). Tannin is the additive that gives wine that 'bite' – without it a wine would appear to be flat and uninteresting (winemakers call it bland). Most red wines have sufficient, the tannin being in the skins of the fruit, but many white wines may need a little – not more than a level saltspoonful of grape tannin powder to the gallon or alternatively a few drops of a liquid tannin solution.

Apart from the fact that tannin helps to bring a wine to 'life', it is also useful as an aid to clarification. In some wines, particularly those in which the elderberry predominates, the tannin content may be unacceptably high, but if this is the case, do not despair, time will result in much of the tannin dropping through, and many a rough young wine has turned out to be first-class after a more prolonged maturation period.

YEASTS

Yeasts are now available to us which greatly encourage the production of good wines. For the beginners perhaps a general

CHART 2
TABLE FOR SELECTING INGREDIENTS
FOR BALANCED WHITE WINES

Using the chart below you can compare the amounts of aroma, acid, tannin and flavour contained in different fruits etc. with the ideal amounts contained in white grapes.

FRUIT ETC	AROMA	ACID	TANNIN	FLAVOUR
White Grapes*	**XX**	**XXX**	**X to XX**	**X to XX**
Apples (cooking)	XX	XX to XXX	XX	XX
Apples (crab)	XXX	XXX	XXX	XXX
Apples (dessert)*	XXX	XX	XX	XXX
Apricots (fresh)	XXX	XX	X	XXX
Gooseberries (cooking)	X	XXX	X	X
Gooseberries (dessert)	XX	XX	X	XX
Oranges	XX	XX to XXX	0 to X	X to XXX
Peaches (fresh)	XXX	XX	X	XXX
Pears (eating)*	XX	X to XX	X to XX	XX
Pears (perry)*	XX	XXX	XXX	XXX
Quince (orchard)	XXX	XXX	XXX	XXX
Rhubarb	0 to X	XXX	XX	0 to X
White Currants	XX	XXX	X	XX
White Grape Concentrate	X	XX to XXX	0 to X	X to XX
Yellow Plums	XX	XX	XX	XX
Cowslip†	XX	0	0	XX
Dandelion†	X	0	0	XX
Elderflower†	XXX	0	0	X
Rose Petal†	XXX	0	0	X

* 100% juice; †1 quart of flowers to the gallon; others 1.8kg (4 lb) per gallon.

purpose yeast may be sufficient, but for those who wish to make wines to type, we now have ranges of yeasts, cultivated from the grapes grown and used in the production of most of the well-known area wines. Given the right ingredients, there is no reason why we should not produce fair copies of many commercial wines (see Charts 4(a) and 4(b)). These special yeasts are available in liquid or granule form, but whichever is chosen, a yeast starter will give the best results, as it will minimise the 'lag period' before the yeast has been able to produce that blanket of carbon dioxide necessary to minimise the possibility of bacterial infection.

Do not be misled into believing any recipe for a 'no yeast' wine. There is no such thing – without yeast there can be no ferment. In these recipes, it simply means that the wild yeasts to be found on the skins of the fruits have been allowed to take over, and the result of this will be a wine that is low in alcohol, and will in all probability be left with off flavours. All fruits should be thoroughly washed before use, and when the wild yeasts have been cleared, then the wine yeast may be added.

SUGAR

We have already touched on the sugar content. Never overdo the sugar in the initial must. It can always be added during the ferment if necessary, but once in, if the yeast is unable to cope, a sweet wine is bound to result. Even if making a sweet dessert wine, it is of considerable advantage if the sugar is added in stages. This enables the yeast to work much better and helps to produce a wine with a stronger alcoholic content. Additional sugar may be added dry, though this does create some problem in dissolving it, or it may be added as invert sugar. This can be made up in batches and added to the fermenting wine as required. It is quite simple to make, and the recipe is as follows:

CHART 3
**TABLE SHOWING THE DIFFERENT TYPES OF ACID
FOUND IN VARIOUS INGREDIENTS**

INGREDIENT			TYPE OF ACID		
	CITRIC	MALIC	TARTARIC	SUCCINIC	OXALIC
Apples		✔			
Apricots	3	1			
Bananas	1	1			
Beetroot	✔				
Blackberries	1	2		*	
Blackcurrants	✔	*			*
Carrots	1	2			
Cherries		✔			
Damsons		✔			
Elderberries	✔				
Figs	✔				
Gooseberries		✔			
Grapes		✔	✔	The proportion varies according to variety	
Grapefruit	✔				
Greengages		✔			
Lemons	✔				
Loganberries	✔				
Oranges	✔				
Parsnips	1	3			
Peaches	1	1			
Pears	2	1			
Pineapples	7	1			
Plums		✔			
Prunes		✔			
Raisins			✔		
Raspberries	✔				
Redcurrants	✔	*		*	
Rhubarb	5	16			2
Sloes		✔			
Strawberries	9	1			
Sultanas			✔		
Tangerines	✔				

✔ indicates the presence of a particular acid.
* indicates that the fruit only contains trace elements of the acid. Where a fruit has more than one acid the numbers show the proportion of each acid to the others e.g. apricots have a 3 to 1 proportion of citric to malic acid.

Ingredients
900g (2 lb) granulated sugar
½ litre (1 pint) cold water
½ tsp citric acid

Method
Place the sugar, 285ml (1 pint) of the water and the citric acid into a saucepan. Bring to the boil, stirring regularly, and simmer for 20 to 25 minutes until it begins to turn to a light golden brown colour. Then add the rest of the water. stir in and leave to cool. This will produce 1.2 litres (2 pints) of invert sugar. So the addition of 150mls (¼ pint) of invert sugar is equal to the addition of 125g (4½ oz) of sugar.

FLAVOUR AND WATER

In our balanced wines there remain two other constituent parts, and these must be inter-related: the fruit (or other ingredient), and the water content. Quantity and treatment of the solids depend entirely on the type used, and at first it might be assumed that the water content should equal the volume of wine produced, i.e. normally eight pints (four and a half litres). However, juices and grape concentrate form part of the eight pints, and allowance for these should be made out of the water to be added, otherwise there may be a tendency for the wine to be thin.

To a certain extent the body of the wine may be helped by the length of time that the solids are left in the fermenting must, but there is a danger that a long aerobic fermentation may extract not only the flavours we want, but also some of the 'nasties' caused by the deterioration of the ingredients or the autolisation of the dead yeast cells. For this reason it is suggested that a period of five days' fermentation on solids should be the maximum – in fact, many experienced winemakers will give a maximum of three days for a table wine, or simply liquidise the must, strain off and ferment solely on the juice. This will certainly give a quicker fermentation, with reduced tannin content in the case of red wines, but there must be a certain loss of body as well, or alternatively an increase in the quantity of fruit used.

VITAMIN B1 AND EPSOM SALTS

Two minor ingredients which will be found in the recipes in this book may appear to be a little unusual to those about to start the hobby. Firstly, the suggested inclusion of vitamin B1 tablets – not essential, but they do aid the yeast, and thereby the fermentation process. Secondly, the addition of a small quantity of Epsom salts (magnesium sulphate) – again by no means essential, but where included, Epsom salts have been found to be beneficial in hardening the water where the supply tends to be rather soft. In hard water areas there is no need for their inclusion.

CHART 4
SHOWING SUGGESTED YEASTS
FOR USE WITH INGREDIENTS MENTIONED

INGREDIENTS	HOCK	SAUTERNES	TOKAY	PORT	MADEIRA	BURGUNDY	CHABLIS	SHERRY	BORDEAUX	CHAMPAGNE	ALL-PURPOSE
Apple	✔	✔					✔				✔
Apricot (dried)	✔							✔			✔
Apricot (fresh)	✔	✔	✔								✔
Banana				✔	✔		✔				✔
Barley				✔				✔			✔
Beetroot					✔						✔
Bilberry				✔		✔					✔
Blackberry			✔	✔		✔			✔		✔
Blackcurrant					✔	✔			✔		✔
Bullace (plum)					✔	✔			✔		✔
Carrot		✔						✔			✔
Cherry			✔	✔	✔	✔			✔		✔
Cowslip	✔	✔								✔	✔
Crab apple		✔								✔	✔
Damson				✔		✔			✔		✔
Dandelion	✔									✔	✔
Date					✔			✔			✔
Elderberry			✔	✔		✔			✔		✔
Elderflower										✔	✔
Fig				✔	✔			✔			✔
Gooseberry	✔	✔	✔		✔		✔	✔		✔	✔

INGREDIENTS	YEAST										
	HOCK	SAUTERNES	TOKAY	PORT	MADEIRA	BURGUNDY	CHABLIS	SHERRY	BORDEAUX	CHAMPAGNE	ALL-PURPOSE
Grapefruit	✔		✔						✔		✔
Loganberry				✔		✔			✔		✔
Mixed Dried Fruit			✔		✔			✔			✔
Mulberry			✔						✔		✔
Orange	✔	✔			✔		✔	✔			✔
Parsley			✔				✔				✔
Parsnip		✔					✔	✔			✔
Peach	✔	✔	✔				✔				✔
Pea-pod			✔					✔	✔		✔
Pear	✔	✔					✔			✔	✔
Pineapple			✔						✔		✔
Plum	✔	✔	✔			✔	✔		✔		✔
Potato		✔									✔
Prune			✔		✔		✔	✔			✔
Raisin	✔		✔		✔		✔	✔			✔
Redcurrant									✔	✔	✔
Rhubarb	✔					✔				✔	✔
Rice			✔						✔		✔
Rose Petal									✔		✔
Wheat			✔					✔			✔

5
TYPES OF WINE

MEAD AND ITS HISTORY

As everyone knows, this is a pleasant alcoholic drink made by fermenting honey and water with yeast. Of all the crafts of our ancestors, mead-making must rank amongst the oldest.

Cave paintings of Stone Age man show the collection of honey from bee colonies, and as it was only necessary to add water to the honey to obtain a ferment from wild yeasts, it seems inevitable that alcohol was discovered this way.

In early Greek civilisation Bacchus was the God of Mead long before becoming the God of Wine. Mead was also offered to the goddess Aphrodite by ladies of good breeding to ensure a plentiful supply of lovers. Well-matured mead was kept for a twice-a-year celebration.

Later the Moors knew mead as a love stimulant, and in fact the deeper one goes into the origins of mead, the more one is convinced not only that it is the oldest drink (known in some form in every ancient civilisation) but also that it always seemed to be connected with, or allegedly have powers in, the field of 'amour'. It is common knowledge that the word 'honeymoon' was derived from the practice of drinking honey-wine during the month-long celebrations which followed better-class weddings.

Though mead, in its simplest form, consisted solely of honey, water and wild yeast, in its more sophisticated form it had various additives, and was known under a variety of lovely names: Melomel, Hippocras, Cyser, Pyment and Metheglin, containing fruit juices, grape and herbs, apple juice, grape, and various herbs respectively. It is from these old recipes that we have gradually developed our country wines.

Although we are inclined to call any honey drink mead, apart from wine mead, there was also a beer or ale mead. In fact the Anglo Saxon word for mead was 'alu', which is close enough to ale to be thought to be a derivation of the word.

The British were never a wine-drinking nation to the same extent as the French or Italians, and in the days when only honey was available as a sweetening agent, beer and ale gradually became the staple drinks. In medieval times, the brewer of bad ale might be put into the 'cucking stool'. This was a chair in which the culprit was made to sit, either at his own door, or in some public place, where the population could see and mock to their hearts' content. Up to the eighteenth century the birth of a child was celebrated in the new father's house, with the fathers of twins sitting at the top table, the fathers of one or more children at the second, and the childless and bachelors at the third (there would be no table-cloth on the third table). This occasion was known as 'sops and ale' and was a great occasion for toasting, eating and drinking. There was certainly an ale-like drink up to the time of the Napoleonic Wars, since trouble occurred in the British Army when the alcoholic strength of the mead supplied to the troops was reduced from 6% to 4%. This was ale strength, and the mead was in fact made with hops and brewers' yeast.

SOCIAL WINES

The present-day definition would probably be a wine with plenty of flavour, too strong in alcohol for a table wine, but not strong enough in either flavour or alcohol for a dessert wine. These wines can be sweet or dry according to taste. In fact, they are classic examples of some of the old country wines, which were made from whatever fruits, vegetables, etc. were available at the time, providing a wine that was suitable for drinking with friends in the evenings. There will be several examples of these social wines in the recipes following, and indeed they form a very useful introduction into winemaking for the beginner.

PURPOSE WINES

With this group of wines we are endeavouring to copy the *type* of wine, and not necessarily a particular commercial wine belonging to the group. We must select our ingredients with greater care with these wines, for it is no use trying to make a dessert wine, for instance, with redcurrants. There is simply not the colour, body or flavour for such a wine. The ingredients must be capable of producing the type of wine we require, and it is hoped that the reader will find the notes against each recipe a help in this respect.

APERITIFS

The definition of these wines is that they should be suitable for drinking before a meal, and should cleanse and waken the palate in preparation for the food to come.

They may be sweet or dry according to type, and although they do not have to be fino sherries or sweet vermouths, this is an indication of what we need. Suitable ingredients for a dry aperitif are parsnips or the citrus fruits, all of which need the addition of sultanas or grape concentrate to give the necessary vinosity. In alcoholic strength they should be at least 16% by volume, and in many instances these wines are lightly fortified, either with vodka or Polish spirit. Most wines of this type are medium to heavy in body, and unless the winemaker is aiming at a sherry, they are often improved by the inclusion of a very small quantity of herbs or quinine. The yeasts used should be capable of working in a high alcoholic wine: Madeira or Tokay yeasts are suitable or Gervin 4 wine yeast or sherry yeast if a dry or sweet sherry is the target.

TABLE WINES

Remember the purpose of these wines is to enhance food, not to dominate it, therefore avoid strong flavours.

RED WINES – Usually light to medium in body, and mostly with a delicate but *good* bouquet – this is very important. These table wines should be dry unless rosé (which should come within the range of 998 to 1004 s.g. on the hydrometer – see Chapter 7). Alcoholic content will rarely exceed 12% by volume, representing a starting gravity of about 1078. Suitable yeasts for the red wines are Beaujolais for the light-bodied wines; Gervin 2, Burgundy or Bordeaux for the medium. Blackberries, elderberries, damsons and red grape concentrate are all suitable ingredients, also blackcurrants in small quantities.

WHITE WINES – Mainly light-bodied, with the exception of white Burgundy in the dry wines and Sauternes in the sweet. Alcoholic content is similar to the red wines, except in the case of a Sauternes type, which should be both heavier in body and in alcohol. Flower and leaf wines would fall into this category, though it must be remembered that all these wines will need to have bananas, sultanas or grape concentrate included in the recipe, otherwise they will be thin and without character. Yeasts suitable for the group of table wines are for the light-bodied, Graves, Hock, Chablis, Champagne, etc. and for the medium wines, Gervin 1, Bordeaux, or Sauternes.

DESSERT WINES

These wines are sweet and full-bodied, and should be fairly strong in flavour. The alcoholic content should be at least 16% by volume, more if possible. In most cases it will be necessary to include at least four pounds of fresh fruit per gallon, and add bananas, raisins or sultanas for increased body. Acidity will be higher than in the other groups, though this will be masked by the sweetness.

AFTER DINNER WINES

This group will include port types, Oloroso sherries, Madeira, etc. and must be full-bodied and even stronger in flavour. They are heavy in alcohol, up to 18% if possible, and are sweet and often fortified. Yeasts suitable are Madeira, Tokay, Tarragona or Gervin 6.

LIQUEURS

Commercial liqueurs can be split into two types – liqueurs and eau de vie.

The first should be made basically from spirits and a flavouring matter such as herbs, fruit, vegetables or flowers added prior to distillation, or alternatively the herbs, fruits etc. are macerated in the spirit for a varying period according to the strength of the additive. In either case the sugar is added later.

The second, eau de vie, are pure distillates made from fruit or vegetable wines, and should not contain any additional flavouring, just sugar to sweeten – examples of these are Framboise (raspberry), Kirsch (cherry), Calvados (apple).

The names of many of these liqueurs have been registered, and we are unable to use them, but there are several firms who are marketing liqueur essences which are very close to commercial types, and it is possible for us to make very acceptable liqueurs with the minimum of effort.

In selecting the wine to be used as a base, do not use your best. The most important thing to remember is that your wine must accept the flavour of the essence, not fight it, and you should therefore look for a mild flavour, but one strong in alcohol. Use a red wine for cherry brandy of course, but a golden wine is suitable for most liqueurs.

For home consumption it is not necessary for you to make the liqueur up to the strength of the commercial equivalent, but this is obviously a matter for the individual. For those who do, I must say that there is one very important piece of knowledge you must have, and that is the working of the 'Pearson Square'. For the purpose of this, let us say that we are endeavouring to make the equivalent of a crème de menthe, and set out the details as follows:

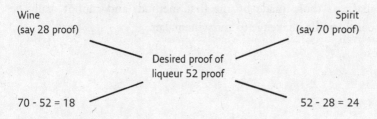

PEARSON SQUARE

Wine
(say 28 proof)

Spirit
(say 70 proof)

Desired proof of
liqueur 52 proof

70 - 52 = 18

52 - 28 = 24

The ratio is therefore 18 parts of wine to 24 parts of spirit
or 3 parts of wine to 4 parts of spirit.

The ingredients for a half bottle would therefore be:

128ml (4½ fl oz) wine
170ml (6 fl oz) spirit (vodka or Polish spirit)
Invert or caster sugar to taste (quantity dependent on the sweetness
    of the wine)
1½ tsp essence
Glycerol to thicken the liqueur

Mix thoroughly. This will be drinkable at once, but it does improve with keeping, particularly as the glycerol does not blend easily.

It is not necessary, however, to copy a commercial liqueur. Why not blend one from your own favourite fruit, herbs, etc.? There are endless possibilities in our country wines – what about the richness of a loganberry or mulberry liqueur? Pineapple? Mint? There is no need to make up a large quantity, just a few fluid ounces to enable you to assess the value of the experiment.

The other method of making a liqueur is probably known to most people: that of steeping fruit in a spirit, adding sugar, and letting Nature do the rest. Such drinks as sloe gin, apricot gin, damson gin, are old favourites, but are certainly not as cheap to make as those made by the first method, and cannot really be considered a challenge to the winemaker.

6
THE PALATE

So now we know what can be done, given the right ingredients and the correct treatment. The majority of beginners will undoubtedly start by making country wines, and their progress will depend largely on the interest the craft creates for them. To make a real success of the hobby, however, there are two more aspects which should be mastered, and these can only be attained with experience.

PALATE TRAINING

The first is palate training, and here a knowledge of commercial wines can be of inestimable value. Why a commercial wine? Because it is at least a standard, in fact the only standard we really have, for the fact that the wine is made for sale means that it has a value, and to a certain extent its price gives an indication of quality. Nowadays many of us are only able to easily sample wines from the lower end of the market, but even so, do take any opportunity of tasting and comparing commercial wines with those produced at home. At first you may feel that your palate is not sufficiently developed to appreciate the finer points, but time will bring about a vast improvement, and this can be speeded up if you happen to be in contact with a group of fellow enthusiasts and can discuss the merits and faults with them.

First of all, then, what is the palate? It consists of three parts – the tongue, the throat and the nose. When we know the principles on which it works, we begin to know which part to use in order to recognise different factors. The golden rule is to try to ignore the obvious and look for the subtleties of flavour and bouquet which will make or mar the wine to be tasted. Sweetness will do much to mask a fault in a wine, but our palates will need to be able to detect the fault if our winemaking is to improve. I always advise anyone to taste the must just prior to the addition of the yeast starter. At first this may not mean very much to the beginner, but gradually it will enable him or her to assess the right acidity and potential flavour.

The tongue is able to detect the presence of bitterness, acid, sugar and salt – B.A.S.S. The top surface of the tongue is covered by up to 9,000 taste buds, each consisting of about 15 taste cells rather like the segments of an orange. Certain areas of the tongue are more perceptive in picking out different flavours:

Front of tongue	Sugar
Left and right outer edges	Salt
Back and back half of sides	Acid
Back of tongue	Bitterness

The tongue, then, should give us a lot of information about the wine we are tasting. But not only have we to recognise these different flavours, but also be able to assess the degree of each.

To obtain the best results it is advisable to have a wine glass which is narrow at the top in order to concentrate the bouquet. A sherry glass would do, but better still a tulip glass or copita, which is the type used by wine judges. The glass should be filled to its widest part, and a good mouthful of wine taken. Whilst the wine is at the front of the mouth and tongue, the degree of sweetness will be most noticeable. The wine should then be allowed to flow round the mouth (it is called 'chewing it') and as it passes the sides of the tongue the acidity will become more apparent. Salt is something which would hardly be found in a wine anyway. As the wine reaches the back of the throat, any bitterness will become apparent, though if this is only very slight, it may only be noticeable when a little of the wine has been swallowed, and the bitterness then comes as a back flavour.

At the top of the nasal system is a region known as the olfactory region which senses a smell and transmits a message direct to the brain. It is not yet established how many types of smell the nose can identify, but obviously with training it is able to tell us what is good in a wine and what is bad. For instance, the 'nose' of a wine which has acetic acid in it and is turning to vinegar will be known before the taste buds ever come into contact with it. When inhaling a wine, take a deep breath, note the inviting (or otherwise) nature of the bouquet, for this impression is a most important one. The nose will also give an indication of the degree of sweetness, vinous quality and balance, though this can on occasions be a little misleading, particularly if the wine is young and yeasty. Constant practice will, however, soon enable you to concentrate on the less obvious aspects of a wine, and give invaluable assistance towards the production of quality wines.

A WINE MEMORY

Whilst this training of the palate is very important, I believe that the second aspect is equally so; that is, for a winemaker at any level to train him or herself to build up a 'wine memory'. It would be useless to taste commercial wines in an endeavour to copy them, or even to use them as a guide, if the lessons learned from that tasting were not remembered and stored away in the memory. Again, this is a long-term project, but once it is mastered it will be of the greatest assistance in blending your own wines in order to bring about the best possible results. Don't worry if progress seems to be slow; a Master Winemaker or National Judge was a beginner once, and possibly years have passed before they have attained these accolades in the craft.

7
USE OF HYDROMETER

I realise that many of those about to take up the hobby have no intention of going to the extra trouble of controlling the alcoholic content, but for those who do, and would ultimately wish to emulate commercial types, the hydrometer and jar become virtual necessities.

A hydrometer is very simple to use. Although it really measures the density of a liquid, it does give us a reasonably accurate indication of the degree of sweetness of a finished wine, and, if used at the beginning and end of the fermentation, an indication of the alcoholic content of that wine. The hydrometer has a bulbous weighted end, and is a tube which is graduated along its length, normally from 990 at the top to 1170 at the bottom. These numbers refer to the specific gravity, and if the hydrometer is placed in a tall, narrow, glass jar which has been filled with water, it will float at a level that gives a reading of 1000. If alcohol is added, a lower reading will result, as alcohol has a lower density than water; but if sugar is added, the reading will be higher, as sugar is of greater density, and the amount of sugar will be indicated. Therefore, if a reading is taken from the must in the bucket just prior to fermentation, that reading will give the total sugar content, i.e. the combination of the natural sugar from the ingredients and the sugar that has been added.

To obtain an accurate reading, the reading should be taken when the temperature of the liquid is at 15.5°C (60°F) and the hydrometer should be given a spin as it is placed in the jar in order to throw off any air bubbles which may be attached. Having taken

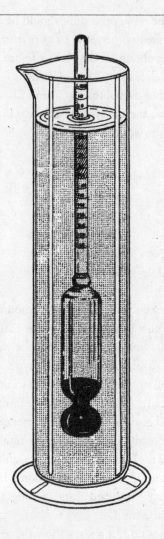

FIG. 2
HYDROMETER AND TRIAL JAR
(floating in water it gives a reading of 1000)

the first reading, the same procedure should be adopted at the end of the ferment. By taking the second figure from the first, the drop in specific gravity is obtained. Divide this figure by 7.36 to find the percentage of the alcohol by volume. Then, if you multiply this percentage of alcohol by volume by 7 and divide by 4, your final answer will give you the proof spirit of the wine. The following is an example of how it works:

First reading	1086	Specific gravity
Final reading	998	Specific gravity
Drop	88	

$88 + 7.36 = 11.96\%$ alcohol by volume
$11.96 \times 7/4 = 20.93$ proof spirit

This, then, is how we learn to assess the amount of alcohol in our wines, and we are now in a position to make table wines, aperitifs, dessert wines, etc. as well as to ensure that the wines finish with the correct amount of sugar content for their type.

The beginner will notice that the recipes in this book sometimes advise that part only of the sugar content or sugar-containing ingredients should be added during the fermentation. Obviously, in these cases the first reading will not give the total sugar content. We get over this problem of assessing the gravity quite simply by taking one hydrometer reading before the additional ingredient is added, another immediately afterwards, and adding the increase to the original gravity of the must.

Commercial wines do not always show the alcoholic content on the label. Even when they do, it can vary quite a lot. An indication of the range of content is as follows:

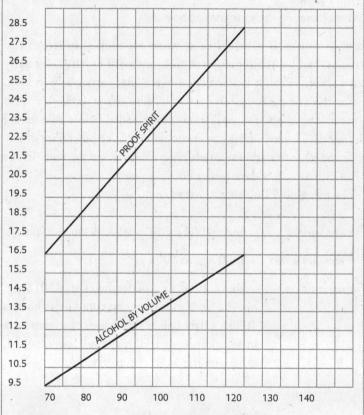

To show percentage of alcohol by volume and proof spirit from any known drop in hydrometer readings.

PROOF SPIRIT

ALCOHOL BY VOLUME

DROP IN HYDROMETER READING

Table wines	– between 10% and 12.5% by volume, except in Sauternes, which may be as high as 14%; German types and rosés are usually amongst the lower percentages.
Aperitfs	– between 12.5% and 16% according to type.
Dessert wines	– 16% and above.

In all instances, it is best if these wines are allowed to ferment to dryness, and be left to mature in this state until required, for a dry wine always matures better than a sweet one, particularly in bulk. Once the wine has matured, a stabilising tablet (available from winemaking shops and online) could be added before sweetening the wine. (The stabilising tablet should avoid the possibility of any re-ferment). After adding a stabilising tablet, leave the wine in the demijohn for a few days before bottling.

The recognised finishing gravities are:

For dry wines	– under 1000 s.g. (if possible down to 990 s.g.).
For medium wines	– 1000 s.g. to 1008 s.g.
For sweet wines	– above 1008 s.g., preferably above 1018 s.g. but if a Sauternes type, this could be as high as 1030 s.g. (though at this degree of sweetness, a little additional acid may well be required, otherwise the wine may tend to cloy).

8
RACKING, PROCESSING AND MATURING

RACKING

Racking is the term used to describe the drawing off of the wine from the deposits of solids and yeast cells (known as the lees) which have accumulated at the base of the fermentation jar. If left, these solids will decompose. When a yeast cell is exhausted and dies, it sinks to the bottom of the jar, where a series of chemical reactions takes place, known as autolysis or self-destruction. Enzymes gradually turn the cell back to its basic constituents, which are released into the bulk of the wine. Some of these constituent parts are then used by the remaining yeast colony, but some are less desirable, and could impart an off flavour in the new wine. It follows, therefore, that the timing of the first racking is of primary importance, and will have a lasting effect on the quality of the wine.

Unfortunately it is very difficult to give fixed periods of time for racking as so much depends on the amount of debris that exists, and the speed of the ferment. A very rough guide would be – first racking after four weeks (always subject to the hydrometer reading indicating a dry wine, or at least a reading down to the degree of sweetness required in the finished wine), second racking after eight weeks, then as necessary at two monthly intervals until the wine is star-bright. Racking does help to clear a wine, but it does also reduce the yeast colony.

When drawing off the wine from the solids, place one end of the rubber tube halfway down the demijohn, suck the other end sharply in order to start the transfer of the wine and then place the tube at the bottom of the receiving demijohn.

Finally a warning – when racking a wine that is not yet stable, do ensure that it has minimum contact with the air. The syphoning tube should go deep into the receiving jar, not allowing the wine to splash. The action of racking will inevitably leave some oxygen in the wine, and an excess of oxygen is liable to cause oxidation, something which although acceptable to a certain extent in a sherry, would ruin a lighter table wine. At this first racking it is advisable to place one crushed Campden tablet to the gallon (four and a half litres) in the receiving demijohn as an insurance against possible oxidation. After subsequent rackings, there will probably be sufficient alcohol to counteract the risk, provided that the above racking instructions have been followed.

PROCESSING AND MATURING

Once our wine has ceased to ferment and has become stable, this is not the end of our endeavours. If winemaking consisted solely of placing set quantities of ingredients in a bucket, and at given intervals, racking and bottling, then our hobby would not retain our interest for long. Louis Pasteur once wrote, 'There is never alcoholic fermentation without the continued life of cells already formed'. When we place the yeast in that bucket, we are helping to create a living thing, for the wine we shall ultimately drink will be changing constantly throughout its life. A complex series of chemical changes takes place, brought about firstly by esters – these are fragrant substances (responsible for the scents and flavours of plants and fruits) which are produced in wines by the action of organic acids on alcohol. Secondly by enzymes, which are lifeless substances produced by the living yeast cells.

Very few winemakers pay enough attention to the important subject of processing and maturing. To make wine, bottle it in about four months, and drink it very shortly afterwards, is all very well, and I do not doubt that your first few gallons will be consumed eagerly, but do try to put away at least one bottle from each batch and allow it to mature fully. As your palate becomes more discerning, you will begin to realise how much better your wines can become by allowing them to mature.

By processing I mean the attention given to the wine at each stage of preparation, particularly in the case of white wines, which should be racked regularly. With the addition of the one Campden tablet at the first racking, your wines will be secure against oxidation and darkening of colour – this is particularly necessary in the case of apples and pears. Always ensure that the fermentation jar is topped up to within 1½ inches (38mm) of the cork after racking, with water or if a light-bodied wine with another similar wine, that airlocks are kept half full (this is usually done with water, but glycerin is even better as it will not evaporate). Also make sure that *all* your equipment is sterilised at all times.

Now for maturation. We are told that wines are best matured in barrels, but this is a luxury that very few of us possess. What is the alternative? Try to mature in bulk if at all possible, in glass jars, or even stoneware jars if you are sure that the glazing is sound. Up to two years for a strong wine, such as a dessert or port; less, probably, nine to twelve months, for table wines. If you are fortunate enough to have a small barrel, keep it for red wines, for these will benefit most from it, but do varnish the exterior first in order to minimise the possibility of oxidation through the wood. If you are maturing in glass containers make sure the corks and bungs fit tightly to exclude the air. It is advisable to cover the jars in some way in order to exclude the light, which particularly with red wines, does affect the colour. A piece of newspaper wrapped round and held in place with a rubber band is quite adequate. Another way is to use brown-coloured demijohns for wines in store, but my objection to this is the difficulty in seeing through the glass in order to find out when a racking is necessary. In all instances a wine will benefit during the maturation period if it can be kept at a steady temperature of just under 60°F (15.5°C).

When bottling time comes round, syphon the wine from the demijohn. Always use a straight cork in preference to one with sloping slides, for if shrinkage does occur, the cork with the sloping sides is more likely to let in the air than one which is touching the neck of the bottle throughout its length. A tip, here, too: when forcing the cork into the neck of the bottle, have a piece of string (about 8 inches/20cm long) partially inside the bottle, but hanging outside. As soon as the cork is inserted, pull out the string, which will then release the air which has been compressed in the neck of the bottle by the insertion of the cork – failure to do this may result in the air pressure pushing the cork out again. There are several types of corking machines available to make the task easy. When the wine is bottled and corked, try to store the bottle at an angle – this will keep the cork moist and thus avoid shrinkage which could let in air.

It is important too, that the finished product should be made as attractive as possible to look at. Never bottle a wine before it is clear enough to drink, for there is nothing worse than being offered a drink from a bottle which has a layer of sediment on the bottom – it is unappetising to say the least, and think of the possibility of off flavours developing from the dead yeast cells which have accumulated in the bottle. Our bottles should be the correct ones for the type of wine they contain; that is, white for a white wine or coloured for a red, though this may be a little difficult at first until an adequate supply has been obtained. The bottles should be thoroughly sterilised before use, the wine star-bright, the cork well into the bottle, and the wine within half an inch (13mm) of the cork.

The labels should be attractive and neatly written, placed equidistant between the seams of the bottle, and sufficiently low that they lie flat – this is particularly important when using

Burgundy-type sloping shoulder bottles. For the few extra minutes it takes, it is useful to add identity details such as the date of making, batch number, and whether sweet or dry. All this information will be of considerable use to you if you are keeping wines for any length of time. Some very decorative labels are available in shops selling winemaking equipment, though these can be quite expensive. If you intend to continue to make wine over a period of years, it is well worth considering the purchase of labels printed from a design you have made yourself. In the long term this can result in quite a substantial saving. The example shown gives the type of wine, batch number, hydrometer reading, alcoholic content, and the date made. In this case, I have a different colour label for each year, which enables me to see the age at a glance. For those who wish to go even further, there are such things as coloured cappings, and neck labels which indicate whether the wine is sweet or dry. All this may seem to be a little unnecessary, but I believe that it is not enough to know you are offering a good wine: it deserves to be *seen* to be at its best.

9
FINING AND FILTERING

Unless they have a bacterial infection, most of our wines will clear to brilliance naturally, but three things will help them to do so:

1. Regular racking.
2. Mild sulphiting.
3. The presence of tannin.

REGULAR RACKING
It may seem strange to say that racking is an aid to clarification, but by watching closely, a further film of yeast and solid deposit will be found at the bottom of the demijohn within two or three days of racking, however clear the wine may seem to be.

MILD SULPHITING
It has been suggested that one Campden tablet should be added at the first racking. This not only minimises the possibility of oxidation, in that it disperses the oxygen which has entered the wine during the racking process, but again it is an aid to clarification.

THE PRESENCE OF TANNIN
The lack of tannin is one of the biggest causes of our winemaking difficulties. Adequate tannin not only gives a better ferment, and a better balance to the wine, but it is also an aid to clarification.

FINING

If we have a persistent haze in a wine, and we have assured ourselves that it is not a pectin or starch haze (see Chapter 10) we still have two methods of attempting to clear it – the first of which is known as fining. However, neither method is as good as Nature's own way, and I would advise its use only if really necessary. I know that many of the commercial kits now on the market provide a fining agent with all their wines, but this is simply to allow the less patient winemaker to obtain the finished product a few weeks earlier, and there is no doubt that some quality is sacrificed in doing this. Among fining agents are the following:

Isinglass – this is a pure type of gelatine, and a one-ounce (28g) packet will fine 10 gallons (45 litres) of wine. Break down the fibres into a powder and dissolve in a cupful of water with a pinch of tartaric acid. This will set in a jelly. Add it to a jug full of wine, mix thoroughly, and add it to the bulk – it is no use adding the isinglass direct to the demijohn as it will not mix easily.

Gelatine – This clearing agent has a positive charge, and should simply be dissolved in hot water, and stirred into the wine. Follow the instructions on the packet.

Albumen (egg white) – one egg will fine 10 gallons (45 litres). Whisk into part of the wine and add to the bulk.

Milk – which contains casein, is another fining agent, and this also has the effect of reducing the colour of the wine. For this purpose, prepare three small clear bottles with about 100cc of wine in each. To the first add ½cc of milk, to the second 1cc and to the third 1½cc. Shake them all thoroughly and leave for 36 hours. From the results you can select the colour you require. Then add the necessary quantity of milk to the bulk of the wine in that ratio.

Because of the difficulties in assessing the quantities required for so small an amount as one gallon (4½ litres), none of these methods is particularly popular with winemakers. Far safer is the use of one of the new proprietary brands of wine finings, the quantity to be used being shown on the containers.

It is most important in using any of these fining agents that the dosage is not exceeded, for this in itself can stabilise the haze, making it impossible for the wine to be cleared to brilliance.

There remains one other lining agent which has the advantage that its use entails no risk of overfining. It is known as *bentonite*, and is a clay which comes from America. One flat dessertspoonful in a cup of wine will be enough to fine a gallon of wine, but it must be mixed very thoroughly before it is added to the bulk. In liquid it tends to swell greatly, but if added to the wine in the correct consistency, it is quick in action and does an excellent job.

FILTERING

If all else fails we can try filtering, but do use this method as a last resort, for it is inclined to take more than just the solids in suspension out of a wine. Many eminent winemakers insist that a wine so treated never recovers in full, and that occasionally the wine will have a slight taste of the filter medium. However, the last few years have seen great strides in the marketing of filtering aids. Up to that time an open funnel and filter paper were all we possessed, and this left the wine in constant contact with the air for lengthy periods with the obvious risk of oxidation. Recently, manufacturers have given considerable thought to the subject, and as a result we now have a number of filtering aids available to us. Most of these exclude the air completely during the filtering process, and are therefore relatively safe, though if using any of them it is advisable to allow the wine to recover before drinking.

10
WINE DISORDERS
AND TREATMENT

In this book I do not propose to go into details of all the wine disorders that can arise, for many occur so rarely that the beginner would be extremely unfortunate to come into contact with them, particularly if the basic instructions on sterilisation have been strictly adhered to. However, there are one or two problems which are fairly common and may be encountered from time to time, and a little knowledge of these and the cure may be of assistance. There are two kinds of hazes which can occur in certain types of wine, both of which can be avoided at the outset if the winemaker has the knowledge.

A *pectin haze* is caused by a gelatinous substance in the fruit (what is good for jam-making often causes problems in winemaking) and the way to avoid this is to use a pectin-destroying enzyme in the must. The use of Pectinol, Pectolase, etc. in accordance with the manufacturer's instructions should prevent a pectin haze forming, but if the finished wine is still hazy, it can be tested for pectin by taking 85ml (3 fl oz) of methylated spirits, 28ml (1 fl oz) of wine, and stirring well. If, after a short while, jelly-like clots or strings begin to form, the haze is caused by the presence of pectin.

The treatment is to add a teaspoonful of Pectolase to the wine, stir well, and keep it in a warm place for a few days, then rack, or filter if the haze does not clear.

The second is a *starch haze*, most noticeable in grain wines. To test for this, place a few drops of the wine on a white plate or tile, and add a few drops of iodine. If the mixture contains black spots or flecks, then starch is present. The treatment is to take 14g (½ oz) of amylase and 85ml (3 fl oz) of water, place it in a bottle and leave for two hours, stirring and shaking it occasionally. Heat the wine to 76°C (170°F) and hold it at that level for twenty minutes. Cool to 38°C (100°F) and stir in the diluted enzyme. In one hour the reaction should be complete. Raise the temperature to 76°C (170°F) again, holding it at that temperature for ten minutes. After cooling, the haze should settle out, and the wine should be racked. All this is quite a lot of work, so to prevent a starch haze forming in the first place, it is far better to add amylase to the must at the rate of one teaspoonful to 4½ litres (1 gallon).

A third common fault found is *flatness or insipidness* in a wine. This is due to the lack of tannin in most cases, and can often be overcome by the addition of a few drops of a proprietary brand of liquid wine tannin solution (obtainable from any winemaking shop) or a cup of cold strong tea to every 4½ litres (1 gallon). Either should be added when the wine is clear, but before maturing. The liquid tannin is preferable as the quantity of tannin is more easily controlled, and a cup of tea does weaken the alcoholic content to a certain extent.

Another of the problems which we sometimes have to face occurs during fermentation. It is known as *acetification*, and with this disorder the wine will gradually turn to vinegar. It is probably the most disastrous disorder, for although it can be stopped if noticed in the very early days, it is often not apparent until it has reached a level when nothing can be done. It can be caused in several ways, by bad storage, the presence of air, the vinegar or fruit fly, or even excessive heat. The last is not often considered, but it should be remembered that the heat in the cap of a must is at least five Fahrenheit degrees higher than the rest of the must. Excessive heat will kill the yeast, but still encourage the growth of bacteria known as Mycaderma Aceti, which will cause this acetification. Those with a keen sense of smell may notice if a wine has a slight tendency towards vinegar. If so, act at once – add two Campden tablets to the gallon (4½ litres) and leave for 24 hours. In the meantime, prepare a yeast starter in a bottle with the same type of yeast used in the original, and when the starter is fermenting, add a little of the wine (but never more than the amount in the starter bottle). Similarly, when this is fully fermenting, add the same amount of wine again, and continue to do this until the whole of the gallon is re-fermenting. Don't forget to sterilise the demijohn that held the infected wine very thoroughly, and also the cork and airlock.

Last, but certainly not least, is the problem that winemakers call a '*stuck ferment*'. This indicates that for some reason the yeast has failed to complete its work, and left us with an over-sweet wine. Stuck ferments are probably one of the more common faults, and may be caused by a number of things:

1 Acetification (which we have already looked into).

2 Excess sugar – this can suffocate the yeast. (But it is not a stuck ferment if the yeast has produced its normal alcoholic content and is still over-sweet. This is an error of judgment on our part in preparing the must).

3 Carbon dioxide in the solution – airlocks should help avoid this, but a good shake up of the demijohn may be of assistance.

4 No yeast – usually caused by over-racking, either too early or too often.

5 Insufficient air – this may seem strange, but 1½ inches (38mm) should always be left between the level of the wine and the cork.

6 Lack of acid – wine may develop an off flavour, but if noticed in time, additional acid may help.

7   Presence of a preservative – this usually occurs when tinned or bottled fruit has been used. Check that tins are marked 'No preservatives', and in the case of dried fruit, ensure that it is thoroughly washed before use.

8   Temperature – either too high, in which case the yeast will have been killed, or too low, in which case the yeast has become dormant. Even an intense fluctuation of temperature can sometimes have the same effect.

9   Lack of nutrients – simply add a further half teaspoonful of nutrient salts.

I cannot close this chapter without giving the beginner some crumb of comfort: don't think that these problems make winemaking an extremely hazardous business – it is not, and with normal luck and adherence to the basic rules. it will only be on very rare occasions in times of trouble that there is any need to look up this section.

11
ENCOURAGEMENT

Those who have just set out on this wonderful hobby of ours deserve all the encouragement winemakers can give them, but apart from advice on a particular problem by an individual, what can we do? What is the set-up throughout the country? The craft of wine and beer making has made great strides in the past 40 years – monthly journals are available, in addition there are books on every aspect, and from a very small beginning at Andover in 1953 has grown a network of clubs, many of which are grouped into area federations. Over all this we have the National Association of Amateur Wine and Beermakers.

Some beginners have taken the first step themselves by joining a wine club, but many hold back under the impression that they will feel lost, out of their depth, and amongst the 'professionals'. How wrong they are. Every club has its quota of beginners, and many hold Beginners' Classes from time to time. I feel sure that most people gain more pleasure in learning the craft in the convivial atmosphere of a wine club, where problems can be discussed with those who have already experienced them, and where there is a social life for the taking. Many club members are content simply to make the occasional gallon in the time-honoured way, and are unlikely to be influenced by competitions, or indeed anything that I may say, but if the newcomer is keen enough, it is possible to progress right up to the stage of becoming a National Judge. Most clubs will hold regular competitions, including Novices' Classes, and although they would obviously like a high percentage of members to take part, it is an accepted fact that many will not do so for one reason or another, and no one should feel bound to enter.

Many clubs are affiliated to their area federations, and it is usual for a federation to hold training classes for senior wine and beer makers, who, after passing written and practical examinations, and proving their ability by suitable competition results, may become Regional Judges. Some of the federations also have their own Masters' Guild, where experienced and qualified members meet to discuss some of the more technical aspects of the craft, and to carry out experimental work, the results of which can be taken back to the clubs. In addition, a federation will hold its own Annual Festival, in which all member clubs may compete, and this is usually followed by a social event in the evening.

Membership of the National Association is open to federations, clubs, and to individual members. The Association exists to further the interests and knowledge of the craft, and to hold an annual competition.

Finally, I must say a few words about that dedicated body, the National Guild of Judges. Membership is by a very strict examination, of course, but members of the Guild always seem available to judge at our festivals, to advise, and to give talks etc. I sometimes wonder how they manage to find time to make any wine or beers for themselves. Without the members of the Guild we would be unable to run these competitions and indeed the standard of our wine and beer making would soon deteriorate.

I have mentioned competitions, which of course exist at all levels, club, federation and national, and although it must be admitted that only a small percentage of members enter, there are many advantages to be gained by those who do. From Novices' Classes in a club competition onwards, there is the pride of achievement, the challenge of beating the existing champion, or simply of gaining points for one's club. Also, practical help is obtained from the advice willingly given by the judges, and by the comparison with other members' wines.

12
RECIPES

All the recipes are for one gallon (4½ litres) unless otherwise stated. In the recipes: tbsp = tablespoon; tsp = teaspoon; dsp = dessertspoon; pt = pint.

The indication of the type of wine against each recipe does not necessarily mean that the yeast will leave the degree of residual sugar associated with that type of wine when it has completed its work. It is simply that the author believes that each recipe will produce the wine at its best if it does contain that amount of sugar. This may well mean that sugar should be added once the wine is stable.

However, when sweetening a wine at the end of a ferment do make sure that the wine is really stable, for any dormant yeast cells can easily restart a ferment when sugar is added – the addition of one stabilising tablet (available from winemaking shops) per gallon should avoid any difficulty. (Of course, if a Campden tablet has been added at the first racking, no stabilising tablet would be needed as the Campden tablet would have killed the yeast). Similarly, when blending one wine with another a restart can occur, and there will almost certainly be a fall-out of minute particles left in the wines, however clear they may seem to be. It is advisable to leave a blended wine in the demijohn for a few days before bottling.

Remember to prepare the yeast starter at least 24 hours before preparing the must.

Remember also that a fermenting wine is best kept at an even temperature, preferably in the range of 65–75°F (18–24°C) – never above.

Do not bottle a wine until is is really clear – any sediment forming in a bottle, either caused by the presence of solids, or dead yeast cells, would be detrimental to the quality of the wine, and apart from this, would result in cloudiness when pouring.

These wines will all improve with keeping beyond the times stated in the recipes.

'Come eat of my bread and drink of the wine which I have mingled'
Proverbs 9, verse 5

RECIPES

57

APPLE

(A MEDIUM-SWEET TABLE WINE)

Bordeaux or all-purpose yeast starter
3.6kg (8 lb) apples
Campden tablets as per instructions
900g (2 lb) granulated sugar
1 litre (2 pints) white grape juice
  (N.B. containing no preservatives)
13mg vitamin B1 tablet
½ level tsp Epsom salts (optional)
1 level tsp nutrient salts
1 level tsp pectic enzyme

1 Obtain a mixture of eating and cooking apples, including, if possible, 450g (1 lb) crab apples. Wash and crush them, either slicing and then pulping them with a block of wood, or better still, putting them through a juice extractor, in which case the quantity could be reduced to 2.5kg (6 lb).

2 Place the crushed apples or juice immediately into a sterilised bucket with 2 litres (4 pints) of water and 1 Campden tablet. After 24 hours dissolve the sugar in 1 litre (2 pints) of hot water, add this and the remaining ingredients, making it up to 4.5 litres (8 pints) with cold water – remember this includes the yeast starter.

3 Ferment in the bucket for 3 days, stirring daily, then strain off the fermenting must into a demijohn under airlock, topping up if necessary.

4   Ferment to dryness in a warm place, and then rack into another jar with 1 Campden tablet.

5   Rack again after a further 14 days.

This wine is drinkable after 3–4 months, but a longer period of maturation will repay, as the wine improves considerably up to 18 months. Sweeten to taste a few days before bottling.

APPLE & ELDERFLOWER
(A DRY, WHITE TABLE WINE)

Champagne or all-purpose yeast starter
800g (13/4 lb) granulated sugar
Campden tablets as per instructions
1 995ml (35 fl oz) bottle of apple juice
  (N.B. containing no preservatives)
2 tbsp elderflower florets
1 3mg vitamin B1 tablet
1 level tsp citric acid
1 level tsp malice acid
1 level tsp nutrient salts
1 level tsp pectic enzyme
285ml (½ pint) white grape concentrate

1 Place the sugar in a sterilised bucket and pour over it 1 litre
   (2 pints) of hot water.

2 Stir until the sugar has dissolved, add 1 Campden tablet and 1.7
   litres (3 pints) of cold water. Then add the apple juice, cover and
   leave for 24 hours.

3 Next day wash the elderflower florets, add them and the
   remaining ingredients (except the grape concentrate) and make
   it up to 4.2 litres (7½ pints) including the yeast starter, with
   cold water.

4 Ferment in the bucket for 4 days, stirring daily, before straining and transferring to a demijohn under airlock, adding the grape concentrate at this stage, and topping up as necessary with cold water. Ferment to a finish in a warm place.

5 Rack as soon as the wine is stable, adding 1 Campden tablet.

This wine is drinkable after 3–4 months. but a longer period of maturation will repay, as the wine improves considerably up to 18 months. Sweeten to taste a few days before bottling.

APRICOT
(A SWEET SOCIAL WINE)

Sauternes or Tokay yeast starter
1.4kg (3 lb) fresh apricots
900g (2 lb) granulated sugar
285ml (½ pint) white grape concentrate
1 heaped tsp pectic enzyme
1 level tsp nutrient salts
1 level tsp Epsom salts (optional)
½ level tsp citric acid
1 3mg vitamin B1 tablet

1   Wash and stone the apricots, mash them and place them in a sterilised bucket in 2 litres (4 pints) of cold water. Add 1 Campden tablet, cover and leave overnight.

2   After 24 hours make it up to 4.2 litres (7½ pints) with warm water. Add the sugar. and stir until it has all dissolved.

3   When the temperature is down to 21°C (70°F) add the remaining ingredients, including the yeast starter.

4   Ferment on the pulp for 3 days, stirring daily, before straining the fermenting must into a demijohn under airlock.

5   Continue the fermentation in a warm place, but watch carefully in case a pulp sediment builds up, in which case rack, even though the fermentation is near complete.

6 Rack again and add a Campden tablet immediately the wine is stable.

7 Store in bulk, if possible up to 12 months. racking as necessary during this time. Sweeten to taste a few days before bottling.

Note: this wine may also be made from dried fruit – if so, use 340g (12 oz) of dried apricots, washed and chopped into small pieces.

BLACKBERRY & APPLE

(A LIGHT-BODIED MEDIUM SOCIAL WINE)

Beaujolais or all-purpose yeast starter
1.1kg (2½ lb) granulated sugar
1.8kg (4 lb) apples (including some crab apples)
Campden tablets as per instructions
1.4kg (3 lb) blackberries
1 heaped tsp citric acid
1 level tsp nutrient salts
1 level tsp pectic enzyme
1 3mg vitamin B1 tablet

Note: taste the fruit beforehand, if it is slightly acid then reduce the amount of citric acid to one level tsp.

1 Place the sugar in a sterilised bucket, and pour 1 litre (2 pints) of very hot water over it. Stir until dissolved, and add 1 Campden tablet.

2 Wash the fruit thoroughly, chop the apples, cutting out all the bad parts. Put the apples into the bucket, liquidise or mash the blackberries in some water and add them also.

3 Cover and leave for 24 hours, and then make it up to 4.5 litres (1 gallon) including 1 litre (2 pints) of hot water.

4 When the temperature is down to 21°C (70°F) add the acid, nutrient salts, pectic enzyme, vitamin B1 tablet and the yeast starter. Stir these in and ferment on the pulp for 5 days, stirring daily, before straining off the solids and placing the liquor in a demijohn under airlock.

5 Top up to 38mm (1½ in) from the base of the cork if necessary with cold water.

6 Continue the fermentation to a finish in a warm place. Rack immediately on completion adding 1 Campden tablet.

This wine should be ready for drinking within 4 months.

BLACK CHERRY
(A SWEET SOCIAL WINE)

Port-type or all-purpose yeast starter
Campden tablets as per instructions
907g (32 oz) tin of black cherries
  (N.B. containing no preservatives)
1.1kg (2½ lb) granulated sugar
227ml (8 fl oz) red grape concentrate
1 3mg vitamin B1 tablet
1 heaped tsp citric acid
1 level tsp nutrient salts
1 level tsp pectic enzyme

1 Pour 1.7 litres (3 pints) of warm water in a sterilised bucket and add 1 Campden tablet.

2 Extract the stones from the cherries and place the cherries and their juice straight into the bucket.

3 Stir in the sugar until it has all dissolved, cover, and leave overnight.

4 After 24 hours make it up to 4.2 litres (7½ pints) with warm water, and when the temperature is down to 21°C (70°F) add the remaining ingredients, including the yeast starter.

5 Ferment on the pulp for 4 days, stirring daily, before straining off the fermenting must into a demijohn under airlock.

6 Continue the fermentation to a finish in a warm place, racking and adding 1 Campden tablet as soon as the wine is stable.

The wine should be ready for drinking between 3–4 months. though it will improve with keeping.

Note: taste the fruit beforehand, if it is slightly acid then necessary to add a little tartaric acid (a pinch at a time) when sweetening to taste before bottling.

BLACKCURRANT
(A SWEET SOCIAL WINE)

Bordeaux or all-purpose yeast starter
900g (2 lb) blackcurrants
1.4kg (3 lb) granulated sugar
Campden tablets as per instructions
227ml (8 floz) red grape concentrate
1 3mg vitamin B1 tablet
1 level tsp pectic enzyme
1 level tsp nutrient salts

1   Wash the blackcurrants. Liquidise or mash them in a little water and place them in a sterilised bucket, together with the sugar and 1.7 litres (3 pints) of hot water.

2   Stir until the sugar has all dissolved, add 1 Campden tablet, cover and leave overnight.

3   After 24 hours, make it up to 4.5 litres (8 pints) with warm water, and when the temperature is down to 21°C (70°F), add the remaining ingredients, including the yeast starter.

4   Ferment on the pulp for 4 days, stirring daily, before straining the fermenting must into a demijohn under airlock.

5 Rack as soon as the wine is stable, adding 1 Campden tablet, and rack a second time after 4 weeks.

6 Sweeten to taste a few days before bottling.

This wine could be drunk after 4 months.

Note: this wine may be a little harsh when young, if so add 2 tsp of glycerin for 4.5 litres (1 gallon) and thoroughly mix before bottling.

CARROT WHISKY
(A DRY OR SWEET SOCIAL WINE)

Sherry or all-purpose yeast starter
1.8kg (4 lb) carrots
800g (1½ lb) granulated sugar (for dry) or
1.1kg (2½ lb) granulated sugar (for sweet)
1 level tsp citric acid
1 level tsp tartaric acid
½ level tsp grape tannin
1 level tsp pectic enzyme
1 level tsp nutrient salts
2 3mg vitamin B1 tablets
285ml (½ pint) white grape concentrate
Campden tablet as per instructions

1 Scrub the carrots, cut them into slices and cook them in 5 pints (2.8 litres) of water until they are soft – do not allow them to mash.

2 Place the sugar, acids and tannin in a sterilised bucket, straining the liquor from the carrots over them.

3 Stir until the sugar has dissolved and allow to cool.

4 When the temperature is down to 21°C (70°F) add the pectic enzyme and leave covered overnight.

5 Next day, make it up to 4.2 litres (7½ pints) with warm water, add the nutrient salts, vitamin B1 tablets and the yeast starter.

6 Ferment in the bucket for 4 days, stirring daily, before transferring to a demijohn under airlock, adding the grape concentrate at this time.

7 Ferment to a finish in a warm place. Even with the higher amount of sugar, the wine may well finish medium to dry, but may be sweetened to taste at the first racking at which time 1 Campden tablet should be added.

This wine may be drunk young but it will benefit greatly from a maturation time of up to a year.

CIDER

Champagne yeast starter
20 lb (9kg) apples
Campden tablets as per instructions
Sugar (as necessary)
1 level tsp nutrient salts

Two things are of vital importance to us in the making of cider: first, the availability of a juice extractor, otherwise the crushing of the apples in order to extract the juice can be a long and messy business, and secondly the blend of apples we use, the best being one third of a sharp cooking apple, one third of a dessert apple, and one third crab apple.

1 Carefully wash the fruit, cutting out any damaged portions, then extract the juice directly into a sterilised demijohn, into which a soluble Campden tablet has been placed.

2 When 4.5 litres (1 gallon) of juice has been obtained, make the gravity up to 1060 s.g. by adding the sugar in 114g (4 oz) batches (see page 47) and stir until the sugar is dissolved, and cover.

3   After 24 hours, add a champagne yeast starter and the nutrient
    salts, and ferment until the gravity has dropped to 1045 s.g.
    then rack and continue the ferment until the reading is down to
    1030 s.g. A further racking at this stage should result in the
    fermentation terminating at around 1020 s.g. – then add 2
    Campden tablets and give the cider a final racking.

The cider may be drunk after 3–4 months.

DANDELION
(A LIGHT, DRY TABLE WINE)

Champagne or Chablis yeast starter
2 litres (4 pints) dandelion flower heads
Campden tablet as per instructions
800g (1¾ lb) granulated sugar
1 heaped tsp citric acid
1 level tsp tartaric acid
2 level tsp grape tannin
1 level tsp nutrient salts
1 level tsp pectic enzyme
285ml (½ pint) white grape concentrate

1 Take 4 ½ litre (one-pint) containers of dandelion flower heads loosely packed, picked on a dry day when in full flower.

2 Remove all the stalks and as much of the green as possible, as this can cause bitterness. Place the flowers in a large container in 2 litres (4 pints) of boiling water.

3 Add 1 Campden tablet and leave them to steep for 48 hours (not more). Then boil the mixture for 10 minutes.

4 Place the sugar in a sterilised bucket, strain the liquor on to the sugar, and stir until dissolved.

5 Make it up to 4.2 litres (7½ pints) with cold water and add the acids and tannin.

6 When the temperature is down to 21°C (70°F), add the nutrient salts, pectic enzyme and yeast starter.

7 Stir well, cover, and ferment for 3 days, stirring daily, before transferring to a demijohn under airlock.

8 As soon as the first heavy ferment is complete (about 5 days) stir in the concentrate, and ferment to a finish in a warm place. Rack as soon as the wine is stable.

This wine can be drunk after 3–4 months.

DATE

(A FULL-BODIED, SWEET SOCIAL WINE)

Madeira or all-purpose yeast starter
900g (2 lb) dates
450g (1 lb) bananas (mashed)
450g (1 lb) granulated sugar
Campden tablets as per instructions
2 level tsp citric acid
1 level tsp nutrient salts
1 3mg vitamin B1 tablet
1 level tsp pectic enzyme
227ml (8 fl oz) white grape concentrate
Invert sugar as required

1 Thoroughly wash the dates in a little water. Chop them up and place them in a sterilised bucket together with the mashed bananas.

2 Add the sugar and 1.7 litres (3 pints) of boiling water, and stir until the sugar has dissolved.

3 Add 1 Campden tablet, cover and leave overnight.

4 After 24 hours make it up to 4 litres (7 pints) with warm water, and when the temperature is down to 21°C (70°F), add the acid, nutrient salts, vitamin B1 tablet, pectic enzyme and the yeast starter.

5 Ferment on the pulp for 5 days, stirring daily, before straining the must into a demijohn under airlock, topping up with the grape concentrate and cold water as necessary.

6 Continue the fermentation in a warm place, and as long as the yeast is working add invert sugar in 142ml (¼ pint) lots each time the gravity drops to 1006. Rack immediately on completion of the ferment, adding 1 Campden tablet.

This wine may be drunk after 4 months.

DATE & GRAPE CONCENTRATE

(A SWEET, HEAVY-BODIED, SHERRY-TYPE WINE)

Sherry yeast starter
1.4kg (3 lb) dates
2 large lemons
2 oranges
450g (1 lb) granulated sugar
28g (1 oz) gypsum
1 level tsp pectic enzyme
1 level tsp nutrient salts
1 3mg vitamin B1 tablet
285ml (½ pint) white grape concentrate
Invert sugar as required

1   Chop, and boil the dates in 3 pts/1.7 litres of water for 30 minutes, together with the thinly pared rinds of the lemons and oranges, carefully avoiding any pith.

2   Place the sugar in a bucket, measure and pour the liquid over it, and stir until it has dissolved.

3   Add the juice of the fruit and the gypsum, make it up to 7½ pts/4.2 litres with cold water, and when the temperature is 21°C/70°F add the pectic enzyme, nutrient salts, vitamin tablet and the yeast starter.

4   Ferment for 4 days, stirring daily, before straining into a demijohn under airlock, adding the grape concentrate. Note: the demijohn is not topped up.

5 Continue the ferment, but add invert sugar in 142ml/¼pt lots each time the gravity drops to 1006. Rack when the fermentation has ceased. This is the only time a sherry-type is racked. Do not top up the airspace. Replace the airlock with a wad of cotton wool.

6 Taste from time to time to ensure the oxidation is not overdone. When ready, replace the cotton wool with an airlock and store in bulk until required.

This wine may be drunk after 6 months.

DATE, SULTANA & FIG

(A SWEET, WHITE DESSERT WINE)

Tokay or Madeira yeast starter
227g (½ lb) dates
900g (2 lb) sultanas
2 3mg vitamin B1 tablets
227g (½ lb) figs
114g (¼ lb) dried bananas
Campden tablets as per instructions
1 level tsp citric acid
1 level tsp nutrient salts
1 level tsp pectic enzyme
1 tin (700ml) white grape concentrate
Invert sugar as required

1   Liquidise in some water or chop the washed dates, sultanas and figs. Put in a bucket.

2   Chop the bananas and boil for 25 minutes in ½ litre/1 pt water.

3   Strain off the solids and add the liquor to the bucket, making it up to 1 litre/2 pts with warm water. Add 1 Campden tablet and cover.

4   After 24 hours make it up to 3.4 litres/6 pts with warm water. When the temperature is at 21°C/70°F add the acid, nutrient salts, vitamin tablets, pectic enzyme and yeast starter.

5   Ferment for 3 days, stirring twice daily.

6 Add the grape concentrate. Ferment and stir for 2 more days.

7 Strain into a demijohn under airlock. Top up with cold water.

8 Each time the s.g. drops to 1010 add 142ml/¼ pt invert sugar.

9 At the end of the ferment adjust the final s.g. to 1040 and add any extra tartaric acid (a pinch at a time) that may be needed.

10 Rack when stable adding 1 Campden tablet. Rack again after a month.

This wine may be drunk after 6 months.

ELDERBERRY (DESSERT)
(A SWEET DESSERT WINE)

Tokay or all-purpose yeast starter
900g (2 lb) elderberries
900g (2 lb) blackberries
114g (4 oz) dates
450g (1 lb) damsons
Campden tablet as per instructions
227g (½ lb) granulated sugar
1 3mg vitamin B1 tablet
10 fl oz (285ml) apple juice (N.B. containing no preservatives)
1 level tsp nutrient salts
1 level tsp pectic enzyme
1 pint (½ litre) red grape concentrate
Invert sugar as required

1 Wash the elderberries, blackberries, dates and damsons. Stone the damsons.

2 Place all the fruit with 2.8 litres/5 pts of warm water in a bucket, add 1 Campden tablet, cover and leave overnight.

3 Stir in the sugar, vitamin tablet, apple juice and nutrient salts.

4 Make it up to 7 pts/4 litres with hot water.

5 When the temperature is 21°C/70°F add the pectic enzyme and the yeast starter.

6   Ferment for 3 days, stirring daily.

7   Add the grape concentrate.

8   Continue the ferment for 2 more days before straining the must into a demijohn under airlock.

9   Each time the s.g. falls to 1010 add ¼pt/142ml invert sugar.

10 Once the wine is stable, rack and raise the gravity to 1030.

11 Store in bulk for a minimum of 6 months – a longer maturation period is even better.

Note: largely dependent on the ripeness of the fruit used, it may be necessary to add a little acid to the wine in order to balance the final sweetness.

ELDERBERRY (TABLE)

(A MEDIUM-BODIED, DRY, RED TABLE WINE)

Burgundy yeast starter
1½ lb (680g) granulated sugar
900g (2 lb) elderberries
2 oz (56g) dates
2 oz (56g) blackcurrants
Campden tablets as per instructions
227g (½ lb) fresh bananas
1 level tsp citric acid
1 level tsp pectic enzyme
1 3mg vitamin B1 tablet
1 level tsp nutrient salts
285ml (½ pint) red grape concentrate

1 Place the sugar and 2 pts/1 litre of hot water in a bucket; stir until dissolved.

2 Remove the stalks from the elderberries and wash them.

3 Wash the dates and blackcurrants.

4 Liquidise the elderberries, dates and blackcurrants in some water or mash them. Add them to the bucket with 1 Campden tablet.

5 Discard the skins of the bananas, chop them into small pieces, and put them in a saucepan in ½ litre/1 pt of water.

6 Boil, simmer for 20 minutes, then strain the liquid into the bucket.

7 Make it up to 2.8 litres/5 pts with cold water, cover and leave for 24 hours.

8 Add 1.4 litres/2½pts of warm water, and when the temperature is 21°C/70°F add the acid, pectic enzyme, vitamin tablet, nutrient salts and the yeast starter.

9 Ferment for 3 days in a warm place.

10 Strain off the solids, add the grape concentrate, and ferment in the bucket for 2 more days.

11 Transfer to a demijohn under airlock; top up with water if needed.

12 Ferment to a finish in a warm place. Rack when the wine is stable and add 1 Campden tablet. A second racking will probably be needed after a further 28 days.

It may be drunk after 4–6 months.

ELDERBERRY & BLACKBERRY

(A LIGHT, DRY, ITALIAN-TYPE TABLE WINE)

Burgundy or Beaujolais yeast starter
570g (1¼ lb) blackerries
170g (6 oz) elderberries
1 large peeled banana
Campden tablets as per instructions
800g (13/4 lb) granulated sugar
1 level tsp nutrient salts
1 level tsp tartaric acid
1 3mg vitamin B1 tablet
1 level tsp pectic enzyme
227ml (8 fl oz) red grape concentrate

1 Wash the fruit. Liquidise it or mash it in 1 litre (2 pints) of cold water.

2 Place it in a sterilised bucket, add 1 Campden tablet, cover, and leave it for 24 hours.

3 Dissolve the sugar in 1.7 litres (3 pints) of hot water, and add it to the fruit, together with the nutrient salts, acid and vitamin B1 tablet.

4 Make it up to 4.2 litres (7½ pints) with cold water and when the temperature is down to 21°C (70°F) add the pectic enzyme and the yeast starter.

5 Ferment on the pulp for 3 days, stirring daily, then strain the fermenting must into a demijohn under airlock, adding the grape concentrate, and topping up as necessary with cold water.

6 Continue the ferment to a finish in a warm place. Rack as soon as the wine is stable, adding 1 Campden tablet, and rack again after another 4 weeks.

The wine could be drunk after 3–4 months.

FIG

(A MEDIUM-BODIED WINE, BEST AS A SWEET SOCIAL WINE)

Madeira yeast starter
680g (1½ lb) dried figs
680g (1½ lb) sultanas
680g (1½ lb) granulated sugar
2 level tsp citric acid
1 3mg vitamin B1 tablet
1 level tsp pectic enzyme
Campden tablets as per instructions
1 level tsp nutrient salts

1   Wash the figs and sultanas thoroughly.

2   Liquidise them in a little water (or chop them) and place them in a sterilised bucket with the sugar.

3   Pour on 1.7 litres (3 pints) of hot water, and stir until the sugar has dissolved.

4   When the temperature is down to 70°F (21°C) add the acid, vitamin B1 tablet, the pectic enzyme and 1 Campden tablet.

5   Cover and leave overnight. After 24 hours make it up to 4.5 litres (1 gallon) with lukewarm water, add the nutrient salts and the yeast starter.

6 Ferment on the pulp for 4 days, stirring daily, before straining off into a demijohn under airlock.

7 Ferment to a finish in a warm place. Rack as soon as the fermentation is complete, adding 1 Campden tablet.

This wine should be sweetened to taste when ready for bottling and could be drunk after 4 months.

FIG & BANANA

(A SWEET SOCIAL WINE)

Madeira or all-purpose yeast starter
900g (2 lb) bananas
900g (2 lb) dried figs
1 level tsp pectic enzyme
1.1 kg (2½ lb) granulated sugar
Campden tablets as per instructions
1 3mg vitamin B1 tablet
½ level tsp grape tannin
1 heaped tsp tartaric acid
1 level tsp nutrient salts

1 Wash the bananas in their skins, then slice them (including their skins) and boil for 30 minutes in 2 litres (4 pints) of water.

2 Wash the figs and liquidise them in a little water (or chop them). Place them in a sterilised bucket with the sugar.

3 Strain the liquor from the bananas, measuring the quantity, and pour it over the sugar and figs.

4 Stir until the sugar is dissolved, add 1 Campden tablet and allow to cool.

5 After 24 hours add the vitamin B1 tablet, tannin, acid, pectic enzyme, nutrient salts and the yeast starter.

6 Make it up to 4.5 litres (1 gallon) with cold water and ferment on the pulp for 5 days, stirring daily.

7 Strain into a demijohn under airlock. and ferment to a finish in a warm place. Rack as soon as the wine is stable, adding 1 Campden tablet.

Note that this wine will probably go dry, and when stable may be sweetened to taste. It could be drunk after 4 months.

FIG, DATE & RAISIN
(A SWEET, FULL-BODIED SOCIAL WINE)

Tokay yeast starter
227g (½ lb) wheat
227g (½ lb) figs
1 ½ lb (680g) dates
1 lb (450g) raisins
900g (2 lb) granulated sugar
Campden tablet as per instructions
1 level tsp pectic enzyme
1 heaped tsp citric acid
1 level tsp malic acid
1 level tsp nutrient salts
1 level tsp amylase
1 3mg vitamin B1 tablet
Invert sugar as required

1 Wash the wheat and soak it overnight in one pt (½ litre) of water to soften it.

2 Next day, strain off and discard the liquid.

3 Thoroughly wash the figs, dates and raisins.

4 Liquidise them in some water or chop them with the wheat before placing them in a bucket.

5 Add the sugar and 3 pts (1.7 litres) of hot water, and stir until the sugar has dissolved.

6 Make it up to 6 pts (3.4 litres) with cold water and add 1 Campden tablet.

7 Cover and leave overnight.

8 Add a further 2 pts (1 litre) of hot water, and when the temperature is 21°C/70°F add the pectic enzyme, acids, nutrient salts, amylase, vitamin tablet and the yeast starter.

9 Ferment for 5 days, stirring daily, then strain the liquor into a demijohn under airlock.

10 Ferment to a finish in a warm place. Rack as soon as the wine is stable.

This is a strong, full-bodied wine, and if it is fed with further quantities of invert sugar at the rate of 142ml (¼ pt) each time the s.g. drops to 1006, it may well become a golden dessert wine. It may be drunk after 6–9 months.

FRUIT JUICE
(A LIGHT, MEDIUM-SWEET TABLE WINE)

Champagne or all-purpose yeast starter
900g (2 lb) granulated sugar
½ litre (1 pint) canned orange juice
½ litre (1 pint) canned apple or pineapple juice
1 level tsp nutrient salts
1 3mg vitamin B1 tablet
1 level tsp pectic enzyme

Note: make sure that the canned juices are free from preservatives.

1 Place the sugar in a sterilised bucket and add 1 litre (2 pints) of hot water.

2 Stir until the sugar has dissolved, and then add the fruit juices, together with the nutrient salts and vitamin B1 tablet.

3 Make it up to 4.5 litres (8 pints) by adding cold water, and when the temperature is down to 21°C (70°F) add the pectic enzyme and the yeast starter.

4 Ferment for 4 days, stirring daily, before transferring to a demijohn under airlock.

5 Ferment to a finish in a warm place, racking as soon as possible after the wine has become stable.

6 Sweeten to taste a few days before bottling.

This wine could be drunk after 3 months.

GINGER
(A SWEET SOCIAL WINE)

All-purpose yeast starter
227g (½ lb) raisins
1.1kg (2½ lb) granulated sugar
114g (4 oz) root ginger
2 oranges
2 lemons
1 level tsp nutrient salts
1 level tsp pectic enzyme
Campden tablet as per instructions

1 Wash the raisins and liquidise them in a little water or chop them.

2 Place them in a large saucepan with 3.4 litres (6 pints) of water.

3 Bring to the boil, add the sugar and the ginger (which should be well-crushed), stir well and simmer for 30 minutes.

4 Pour this into a sterilised bucket, measuring the quantity of liquid left after boiling.

5 Make it up to 4.5 litres (8 pints) with cold water, and add the juice of the oranges and lemons, and the thinly peeled rinds, carefully avoiding any of the white pith.

6 Add the nutrient salts, and when the temperature is down to 21°C (70°F) add the pectic enzyme and the yeast starter.

7 Ferment on the pulp for 5 days, stirring daily, before straining into a demijohn under airlock.

8 Ferment to a finish in a warm place, racking as soon as the wine is stable.

9 Add 1 Campden tablet and sweeten to taste.

This wine may be drunk after 4 months.

GOOSEBERRY
(A GERMAN-TYPE MEDIUM TABLE WINE)

Hock yeast starter
450g (1 lb) granulated sugar
900g (2 lb) green gooseberries
1 level tsp tartaric acid
227g (½ lb) sultanas
1 3mg vitamin B1 tablet
Campden tablets as per instructions
1 level tsp nutrient salt
995ml/35 fl oz apple juice (N.B. containing no preservatives)
1 level tsp pectic enzyme
1 tbsp elderflowers
114g (4 oz) clear honey

1   Wash the fruit. Liquidise (or chop or mash) it in a little water.

2   Place it in a sterilised bucket with 1 Campden tablet.

3   Add the apple juice, a pint (½ litre) of water, and cover.

4   After 24 hours place the honey in a saucepan with ½ litre (1 pint) of water and bring to the boil.

5   Add this, together with another pint (½ litre) of hot water, to the bucket.

6   Add the sugar, acid, vitamin B1 tablet, and stir until the sugar has dissolved.

7   Make it up to 4.5 litres (1 gallon) by adding cold water, and when the temperature is down to 21°C (70°F) add the nutrient salts, pectic enzyme and yeast starter.

8   Ferment on the pulp for 2 days, stirring twice a day, before straining into a second sterilised bucket and adding the elderflowers.

9   After a further 2 days the liquor should be transferred to a demijohn under airlock and the fermentation continued to completion in a warm place.

10 Carry out the first racking when the gravity is down to 1006. adding 1 Campden tablet, and rack again 28 days later.

This wine could be drunk after 3–4 months.

GRAPE
(A MEDIUM-DRY, CHIANTI-TYPE, RED TABLE WINE)

Very few of us have the opportunity of producing a wine solely from the fresh grape, so this gives me the chance to introduce a wine which is *really* for the beginner – in other words, from a commercially-produced tin of concentrated grape juice. There are many brands on the market now, producing red, white, sherry-type etc. wines and to endeavour to draw comparisons would be difficult.

I have selected this wine, made from a tin of light dry red concentrate, and you should have no problem in obtaining this from any winemaking shop or online. Normally full instructions are found on the reverse of the label, and the making of the wine is simplicity itself. Fermentation is generally started in the sterilised demijohn under airlock with about 2.8 litres (5 pints) of water and the contents of the tin, with a few ounces of sugar added at 2 stages during the ferment. After the first 4 or 5 days (or when the heavy ferment has subsided) the demijohn is topped up with water.

Obviously racking is easy, as it is only the dead yeast cells which have to be removed, and some brands of these concentrates even include wine finings, which will clear the wine within a few days, thereby making it drinkable much earlier. It must be pointed out, however, that it does not 'mature' quicker, and it will still be greatly improved if nature is allowed to take her own time.

If a packet of yeast is not included, I would suggest a Burgundy or Beaujolais yeast for this type of wine.

GRAPE & HONEY

(A MEDIUM-BODIED, WHITE TABLE WINE)

Hock or all-purpose yeast starter
340g (12 oz) clover honey
1 tin (700ml) white grape concentrate (medium or dry type)
2 3mg vitamin B1 tablets
½ level tsp citric acid
1 level tsp nutrient salts
1 level tsp pectic enzyme
Campden tablet as per instructions

1. Place the honey in a saucepan in 1 litre (2 pints) of water, bring to the boil, and allow to cool.

2. Pour the white grape concentrate into a demijohn and add 1.7 litres (3 pints) of warm water, swilling out the can to ensure that all the concentrate is used.

3. Add the boiled honey and make it up to 4.5 litres (1 gallon) with cold water.

4. Add the remaining ingredients including the yeast starter when the temperature is down to 21°C (70°F).

5. Ferment for 5 days, shaking the jar daily, before topping up with cold water.

6. Ferment to a finish in a warm place, racking immediately the wine is stable, and add 1 Campden tablet.

The wine should ferment to medium-dry, and may be sweetened to taste. It could be drunk after 3–4 months.

GRAPEFRUIT
(A DRY APERITIF WINE)

Tokay yeast starter
9 small grapefruits
Campden tablets as per instructions
340g (12 oz) sultanas
1 level tsp pectic enzyme
1 level tsp nutrient salts
1 3mg vitamin B1 tablet
1.1kg (2½ lb) sugar

1 Cut the grapefruits in half, extract the juice, and place it in a sterilised bucket with 1 soluble Campden tablet.

2 After 24 hours wash the dried fruit thoroughly. Liquidise it in a little water or chop it, and add it to the juice, together with the pectic enzyme, nutrient salts, vitamin B1 tablet and 680g (1½ lb) of the sugar.

3 Make it up to 3.4 litres (6 pints) with tepid water, add the yeast starter, cover and ferment on the pulp for 3 days, stirring daily.

4 Strain off the solids and place the liquor in a demijohn under airlock.

5 Agitate the jar twice daily for the next 2 days, then add the remaining 450g (1 lb) of sugar. Again agitate the jar until the sugar has dissolved, and top up with cold water.

6 Ferment to dryness in a warm place, racking immediately the wine is stable, and adding 1 Campden tablet.

At its best this is a long-term wine, maturing for up to 18 months in bulk, but it is quite pleasant as a younger wine if sweetened to taste a few days before bottling.

GREENGAGE & SULTANA

(A MEDIUM-DRY, WHITE TABLE WINE)

Bordeaux or all-purpose yeast starter
1.8kg (4 lb) greengages
900g (2 lb) sultanas
450g (1 lb) granulated sugar
Campden tablets as per instructions
1 3mg vitamin B1 tablet
1 level tsp nutrient salts
1 level tsp pectic enzyme
285ml (½ pint) yellow rose petals (loosely packed)

1   Wash and stone the greengages. Discard the stones.

2   Wash the sultanas.

3   Liquidise the sultanas and greengages in a little water or chop them. Place them in a sterilised bucket with the sugar.

4   Pour 2.8 litres (5 pints) of boiling water over them, add 1 Campden tablet, and stir until all the sugar has dissolved. Cover and leave overnight.

5   After 24 hours make it up to 4.5 litres (8 pints) with warm water, and when the temperature is down to 21°C (70°F) add the vitamin tablet, nutrient salts, pectic enzyme and yeast starter.

6 Ferment on the pulp for 3 days, stirring daily, before straining off the solids into a second bucket and adding the rose petals.

7 After a further 2 days strain the liquor into a demijohn under airlock, and ferment to a finish in a warm place.

8 Rack as soon as the wine is stable, adding a Campden tablet, and rack a second time within 4 weeks. Store in a cool place for the maturation period.

This wine could be drunk after 3–4 months.

LEMON BALM

(A LIGHT, DELICATE, MEDIUM-SWEET TABLE WINE)

Champagne or all-purpose yeast starter
1 litre (2 pints) lemon balm leaves
  (with no stalks, loosely packed)
Campden tablet as per instructions
450g (1 lb) sultanas
738ml (1 26 fl oz) bottle of grape juice
  (N.B. containing no preservatives)
1020g (2½ lb) granulated sugar
1 3mg vitamin B1 tablet
½ level tsp citric acid
½ level tsp tartaric acid
1 level tsp pectic enzyme
1 level tsp nutrient salts

1 Wash the lemon balm leaves in running water. and place them
   in a sterilised bucket. Pour 2 litres (4 pints) of boiling water over
   them, add 1 Campden tablet, cover, and leave for 48 hours,
   stirring twice daily.

2 Wash the suitanas. Liquidise them in a little water or chop
   them. Add them, the grape juice and the sugar to the bucket.

3 Make it up to 4.5 litres (1 gallon) with hot water, stir until the
   sugar has dissolved, and when the temperature is down to 21°C
   (70°F) add the remaining ingredients, including the yeast starter.

4 Cover and ferment on the pulp for 3 days, stirring daily, before straining off and placing the liquor into a demijohn under airlock.

5 Continue the fermentation to completion in a warm place. Rack as soon as the wine is stable, and a second time within 28 days.

This wine could be drunk after 3 months.

MAIZE
(A SWEET SOCIAL WINE)

Cereal or all-purpose yeast starter
680g (1½ lb) maize (off the cob)
1.4kg (3 lb) granulated sugar
Campden tablets as per instructions
Juice of two oranges
1 level tsp amylase
2 3mg vitamin B1 tablets
½ level tsp grape tannin
1 level tsp citric acid
1 level tsp tartaric acid
1 level tsp nutrient salts
285ml (½ pint) white grape concentrate

1   Soak the maize in 2 pints (1 litre) of water overnight. Discard
    the liquid and place the maize in a sterilised bucket with the
    sugar.

2   Add 2 pints (1 litre) of hot water and stir until the sugar has
    dissolved.

3   Make it up to 2.8 litres (5 pints) with cold water, add 1
    Campden tablet, the juice of the oranges and the amylase, and
    leave for 24 hours.

4   Add the vitamin B1 tablets, tannin, acids, nutrient salts,
    together with 1.4 litres (2½ pints) of warm water.

5 When the temperature is down to 21°C (70°F) add the yeast starter, and ferment on the pulp for 4 days, stirring daily, before straining into a demijohn under airlock.

6 At this stage add the grape concentrate, and if necessary top up with cold water. Continue the fermentation to a finish in a warm place. If the ferment is prolonged, rack once the specific gravity drops to 1020 and add a Campden tablet.

Note: as with all grain wines, a long maturation period of at least 12 months is advisable, for a young wine tends to be harsh. The addition of 2 teaspoonsful of glycerin helps to smooth a young grain wine.

MEAD (PYMENT)
(A DRY SOCIAL WINE)

Hock or Champagne yeast starter
1.4kg (3 lb) clover honey
Campden tablets as per instructions
738ml (1 26 fl oz) bottle of grape juice
  (N.B. containing no preservatives)
1 heaped tsp nutrient salts
½ level tsp Epsom salts (optional)
2 3mg vitamin B1 tablets
½ level grape tannin
1 level tsp malic acid
1 heaped tsp tartaric acid

Note: if a sweeter wine is desired, add another 450g (1 lb) of honey to this recipe.

1 Place the honey in 1.7 litres (3 pints) of water in a saucepan, stir well, and bring to the boil. Then place it in a sterilised bucket, make it up to 4 litres (7 pints) with cold water and add 1 Campden tablet.

2 Cover and leave for 24 hours, before adding all the remaining ingredients, including the yeast starter.

3 Ferment in the bucket for 4 days, stirring daily, before transferring to a demijohn under airlock.

4   Ferment to dryness in a warm place, then rack, add a Campden tablet and top up with cold water.

5   Allow to mature in a cool place, giving the wine a second racking after about 3 months.

This is not a quick maturing wine, and will improve greatly with keeping. If it is kept for a longer period, rack during maturation at four-monthly intervals.

MINT

(A LIGHT, DRY TABLE WINE)

Chablis or all-purpose yeast
852ml (1½ pints) mint leaves
  (lightly bruised and loosely packed)
227g (½ lb) sultanas
1020g (2¼ lb) granulated sugar
Campden tablets as per instructions
1 3mg vitamin B1 tablet
½ level tsp grape tannin
1 heaped tsp nutrient salts
1 level tsp pectic enzyme

1 Wash the mint leaves thoroughly and place them in a sterilised bucket.

2 Wash the sultanas. Liquidise them in a little water or chop them. Add them, with the sugar, to the bucket, together with 2.8 litres (5 pints) of boiling water.

3 Add 1 Campden tablet, cover, and leave for 24 hours.

4 Add a further 1.7 litres (3 pints) of hot water, and when the temperature is down to 21°C (70°F) add the remaining ingredients, including the yeast starter.

5 Ferment on the pulp for 3 days, stirring twice daily, and then strain the liquor into a second sterilised bucket.

6 After a further 2 days, transfer to a demijohn under airlock, and ferment to a finish in a warm place.

7 Rack as soon as possible once the wine is stable, adding a Campden tablet. A second racking will probably be required within 28 days.

This wine could be drunk after 3–4 months.

MIXED DRIED FRUIT
(A MEDIUM-BODIED SOCIAL WINE)

Tokay or all-purpose yeast starter
450g (1 lb) wheat
450g (1 lb) sultanas
227g (½ lb) raisins
227g (½ lb) figs
900g (2 lb) granulated sugar
2 level tsp citric acid
1 level tsp nutrient salts
1 level tsp pectic enzyme
1 3mg vitamin B1 tablet
Campden tablet as per instructions

1 Wash the wheat well and soak it overnight in ½ litre (1 pt) of water.

2 Strain and discard the liquid. Wash the dried fruit.

3 Liquidise it with the wheat in some water, or bruise the wheat and chop the dried fruit.

4 Place the dried fruit, wheat, sugar and acid in a bucket.

5 Add 1 litre (2 pts) of boiling water. Stir until the sugar has dissolved. Make it up to 4.5 litres (8 pts) with cold water.

6 When the temperature is 21°C/70°F add the nutrient salts, pectic enzyme, vitamin tablet and the yeast starter.

7 Cover, and ferment for 5 days, stirring daily.

8 Strain into a demijohn under airlock. Ferment to a finish in a warm place. Rack as soon as the wine is stable, adding 1 Campden tablet.

Note: this wine should be medium to dry at the end of the ferment. For a sweeter wine, sweeten to taste a few days before bottling; if necessary also add tartaric acid (a pinch at a time) to keep the wine in balance. If alcoholic strength is important, 142ml/¼ pt invert sugar may be added when the s.g. drops to 1006; remember the wine will become sweeter as the alcohol content rises.

It may be drunk after 4–6 months.

OAK LEAF

(A LIGHT, DRY TABLE WINE)

Chablis or all-purpose yeast starter
4.5 litres (1 gallon) young oak leaves
  (loosely dropped into the container)
900g (2 lb) granulated sugar
227ml (8 fl oz) white grape concentrate
2 3mg vitamin B1 tablets
Juice of 1 orange
1 level tsp tartaric acid
1 level tsp citric acid
1 level tsp pectic enzyme
1 level tsp nutrient salts

1 Wash the oak leaves in cold water and place them in a sterilised bucket. Pour 2 litres (4 pints) of boiling water over them, cover, and leave for 24 hours.

2 Strain off the liquid into a second bucket, add the sugar and a further 1 litre (2 pints) of hot water and stir until the sugar has dissolved.

3 Make it up to 4.5 litres (8 pints) with cold water, and when the temperature is down to 21°C (70°F) add the remaining ingredients, including the yeast starter.

4 Ferment for 4 days, stirring daily, before transferring to a demijohn under airlock.

5 Top up as necessary, and ferment to a finish in a warm place. Rack as soon as the wine is stable, and mature in a cool place.

Note: the addition of 2 tsp of glycerin added to the demijohn before bottling, i.e. during the maturation period, will improve this wine.

The wine could be drunk after 3–4 months.

ORANGE

(A MEDIUM OR SWEET TABLE WINE)

Sauternes or all-purpose yeast starter
12 sweet medium-sized oranges
1.1kg (2½ lb) granulated sugar
1 3mg vitamin B1 tablet
1 level tsp pectic enzyme
1 level tsp nutrient salts
Campden tablet as per instructions

1 Wash the oranges and peel 6 of them thinly, carefully avoiding the white pith.

2 Place the sugar in a sterilised bucket and pour in 1.7 litres (3 pints) of boiling water. Stir until the sugar has dissolved, and then add the peel ofthe 6 oranges.

3 Cover and leave overnight, and then add the juice from all 12 oranges.

4 Make it up to 4.5 litres (8 pints) with warm water, and when the temperature is down to 21°C (70°F) add the remaining ingredients, including the yeast starter.

5 Ferment for 5 days, stirring daily, before straining into a demijohn under airlock.

6 Ferment to completion in a warm place. Rack as soon as the wine is stable, adding 1 Campden tablet, and rack a second time within 28 days.

7 Sweeten to taste a few days before bottling, but watch the acidity; it may be necessary to add a little acid to balance the sugar.

This wine could be drunk after 4 months.

ORANGE (SEVILLE)

(A SWEET APERITIF-TYPE WINE)

Champagne or all-purpose yeast starter
8 small Seville oranges
1.1kg (2½ lb) granulated sugar
Campden tablets as per instructions
1 3mg vitamin B1 tablet
1 level tsp nutrient salts
1 level tsp pectic enzyme
227ml (8 fl oz) white grape concentrate

1   Wash the oranges and peel 4 of them very thinly, taking care not to include any of the white pith.

2   Boil the peel for 20 minutes in a pint (½ litre) of water, cover, and leave it for 24 hours in order to extract the zest.

3   Peel the remaining 4 oranges.

4   Extract the juice from all the oranges. Place this juice, the thinly cut peel from the 4 oranges, the juice and water (from the saucepan) and the sugar, into a sterilised bucket.

5   Pour in 2 pints (1 litre) of boiling water and stir until the sugar has dissolved. Add 1 Campden tablet, cover, and leave for 24 hours.

6 Make it up to 4.2 litres (7½ pints) with cold water, add the vitamin B1 tablet, nutrient salts, pectic enzyme, and stir in the yeast starter.

7 Cover, and ferment for 4 days, stirring daily, before straining into a demijohn under airlock, adding the grape concentrate and topping up with cold water as necessary.

8 Ferment to a finish in a warm place. Rack as soon as the wine is stable and add 1 Campden tablet.

Note: this wine will take some time to mature, for at first it will be inclined to be bitter. Time will mellow this, and when it is finally ready (probably after 6 months) it can be sweetened to taste.

PARSLEY
(A LIGHT, DRY TABLE WINE)

Chablis or all-purpose yeast starter
227g (8 oz) parsley heads
227g (8 oz) granulated sugar
1 tin (700ml/24½ fl oz) white grape concentrate (dry)
1 level tsp pectic enzyme
1 level tsp nutrient salts
1 3mg vitamin B1 tablet
Campden tablet as per instructions

1   Wash the parsley and discard the stalks. Place the remainder in a saucepan with 2 litres (4 pints) of water, bring to the boil, and simmer for 15 minutes.

2   Place the sugar in a sterilised bucket, and strain the water from the parsley over it.

3   Stir until the sugar has dissolved, cover, and allow to cool – when the temperature is down to 21°C (70°F) add the grape concentrate and remaining ingredients, including the yeast starter.

4 Make it up to 4.5 litres (8 pints) by adding cold water, and ferment in the bucket for 5 days before transferring to a demijohn under airlock, topping up with cold water as necessary.

5 Ferment to a finish in a warm place, racking as soon as the wine is stable, and adding 1 Campden tablet.

This wine could be drunk after 4 months.

PARSNIP
(A LIGHT, MEDIUM-SWEET TABLE WINE)

Sauternes or all-purpose yeast starter
1.8kg (4 lb) parsnips
2 oranges
1.1kg (2½ lb) granulated sugar
227g (½ lb) sultanas
Campden tablets as per instructions
1 level tsp pectic enzyme
1 3mg vitamin B1 tablet
1 heaped tsp citric acid
1 level tsp nutrient salts

This is best made towards the end of the winter months.

1 Scrub, slice the parsnips and place in a pan containing 6 pts (3.4 litres) of water.

2 Add the thinly peeled skins of the oranges, being careful to avoid any of the pith.

3 Boil, and simmer for 10 minutes – never more, or the finished wine may have a haze.

4 Strain off the liquid into a bucket containing the sugar, taking note of the amount of liquid. Stir until the sugar has dissolved.

5 Wash the sultanas. Liquidise them in some water or chop them, and add them, together with the juice of the oranges, again taking note of the amount.

6 Make it up to 4.5 litres (8 pts) with cold water, add 1 Campden tablet and cover.

7 After 24 hours add the pectic enzyme and the remaining ingredients, including the yeast starter.

8 Ferment for 4 days, stirring daily.

9 Strain into a demijohn under airlock. Continue the fermentation in a warm place until the s.g. is down to 1006, then rack and add 1 Campden tablet.

10 Allow the ferment to continue to completion. Should the wine go down to dryness, it may be sweetened a few days before bottling.

This wine may be drunk after 6 months.

PEACH
(A SWEET, WHITE TABLE WINE)

Tokay or Sauternes yeast starter
1020g (2¼ lb) granulated sugar
425g (115 oz) tin peaches (N.B. containing no preservatives)
1 3mg vitamin B1 tablet
½ level tsp grape tannin
2 level tsp pectic enzyme
1 heaped tsp citric acid
1 level tsp tartaric acid
1 level tsp nutrient salts
227ml (8 fl oz) white grape concentrate
Campden tablet as per instructions

1 Place the sugar in a sterilised bucket and pour on 1.7 litres (3 pints) of hot water.

2 Stir until the sugar has dissolved, then add the peaches, chopping them as small as possible.

3 Make it up to 7½ pints (4.2 litres) with cold water, and when the temperature is down to 21°C (70°F) add all the ingredients except the grape concentrate.

4 Ferment on the pulp for 4 days, stirring daily, then strain the fermenting must into a demijohn under airlock, adding the concentrate and topping up as necessary.

5 Ferment to a finish in a warm place, racking as soon as the wine is stable and adding 1 Campden tablet.

6 Rack again within 28 days.

This wine may well go down to dryness, and once it is stable, it should then be sweetened to taste – probably to about 1024 s.g.

The wine could be drunk after 3–4 months.

PEA-POD

(A DELICATE, MEDIUM-SWEET, LIGHT TABLE WINE)

Bordeaux or all-purpose yeast starter
2.3kg (5 lb) fresh pea-pods (not the peas)
1.4kg (3 lb) granulated sugar
227g (½ lb) sultanas
Campden tablets as per instructions
1 3mg vitamin B1 tablet
2 tsp citric acid (1 heaped, 1 level)
½ level tsp grape tannin
1 level tsp nutrient salts

1   Wash the pods carefully, and boil them in 6 pints (3.4 litres) of water until tender, then strain the liquor into a sterilised bucket.

2   Add the sugar, and stir until it has dissolved. Wash the sultanas. Liquidise them in a little water or chop them, and place them in the bucket.

3   Add 1 Campden tablet, cover, and leave for 24 hours.

4   Add the remaining ingredients, and ferment on the pulp for 3 days, stirring daily, before straining the fermenting must into a demijohn under airlock.

5 Make it up to 4.5 litres (8 pints) by adding cold water as soon as the heavy ferment subsides.

6 Ferment to a finish in a warm place, adding a Campden tablet at the first and second rackings.

This wine could be drunk after 3–4 months.

PEAR
(A LIGHT TABLE WINE, BEST MEDIUM-SWEET)

Champagne or all-purpose yeast starter
Campden tablets as per instructions
1.8kg (4 lb) pears
900g (2 lb) granulated sugar
1 3mg vitamin B1 tablet
1 level tsp pectic enzyme
1 level tsp nutrient salts
1 heaped tsp citric acid
227ml (8 fl oz) white grape concentrate

1 Put 1.7 litres (3 pints) of tepid water in a sterilised bucket and add 1 Campden tablet.

2 Wash the pears, chop, and place them immediately into the bucket. (This is in order to avoid oxidation.)

3 Cover and leave overnight. After 24 hours, make it up to 6 pints (3.4 litres) with warm water, add the sugar and stir until it has dissolved.

4 When the temperature is down to 21°C (70°F) add the remaining ingredients (including the yeast starter) with the exception of the grape concentrate, and ferment on the pulp for 3 days, stirring daily.

5 Strain the fermenting must into a demijohn under airlock, and after a further 2 days, add the grape concentrate and make it up to 4.5 litres (1 gallon) with cold water.

6 Ferment to a finish in a warm place, and rack as soon as the wine is stable, adding 1 Campden tablet.

7 Rack a second time within 21 days.

The wine may be sweetened to taste a few days before bottling and it may be necessary to adjust the acid level if the pears used were very ripe. The wine could be drunk after 3–4 months.

PINEAPPLE & GRAPE

(A LIGHT, MEDIUM-SWEET WINE)

Champagne yeast starter
435g (215 oz) tins pineapple in syrup, or pulp
  (N.B. containing no preservatives)
2 pints (l litre) white grape juice
  (N.B. containing no preservatives)
1020g (2½ lb) granulated sugar
1 heaped tsp citric acid
½ level tsp grape tannin
1 level tsp nutrient salts
1 level tsp pectic enzyme

1 Finely chop the pineapple and place it and its syrup in a
   sterilised bucket together with the white grape juice and the
   sugar.

2 Pour in 1 litre (2 pints) of boiling water and stir until the sugar
   has dissolved.

3 Add 2 litres (4 pints) of cold water and when the temperature is
   down to 70°F (21°C) add the remaining ingredients, including
   the yeast starter.

4 Cover, and ferment on the pulp for 3 days, stirring daily, before
   straining the must into a demijohn under airlock, topping up
   with cold water if necessary.

5 Continue the fermentation in a warm place, racking as soon as the wine is stable.

6 This wine will be drinkable in 3 months, but will improve if kept a little longer.

Note: for a heavier wine, add another tin of pineapple and a further 450g (1 lb) of sugar.

PLUM
(A SWEET, WHITE SOCIAL WINE)

Sauternes or all-purpose yeast starter
Campden tablet as per instructions
1.8kg (4 lb) golden plums
1.1kg (2½ lb) granulated sugar
1 3mg vitamin B1 tablet
1 heaped tsp pectic enzyme
1 level tsp nutrient salts
1 level tsp citric acid
227ml (8 fl oz) white grape concentrate

1 Put 1.7 litres (3 pints) of tepid water in a sterilised bucket and add 1 Campden tablet.

2 Wash, stone the plums and discard the stones. Place the plums immediately into the bucket.

3 Cover and leave for 24 hours.

4 Add 1.7 litres (3 pints) of hot water and the sugar. Stir until the sugar has dissolved.

5 Make it up to 3.4 litres (6 pints) by adding cold water and add the remaining ingredients except the grape concentrate.

6 Ferment on the pulp for 4 days, stirring daily, before straining off the fermenting must into a demijohn under airlock, and adding the grape concentrate.

7 Top up with 4.5 litres (1 gallon) as soon as the first heavy ferment subsides, and continue the fermentation in a warm place to dryness.

8 Rack as soon as the wine is stable, and again after a further 3 weeks, adding a Campden tablet at each racking.

9 Mature for 6 months to obtain the best results, sweetening to taste a few days before bottling,

Note: by the substitution of damsons for the golden plums, and red concentrate for white, a rich sweet red social wine can be made.

PORT-TYPE

(A FULL-BODIED, SWEET DESSERT WINE)

Port or Gervin 6 yeast starter
114g (4 oz) dried bananas
680g (1½ lb) granulated sugar
1.4kg (3 lb) elderberries, stripped
900g (2 lb) blackberries
4 oz (114g) raspberries
Campden tablets as per instructions
450g (1 lb) bilberries (bottled – no preservatives)
1 level tsp citric acid
1 level tsp pectic enzyme
1 level tsp nutrient salts
1 3mg vitamin B1 tablet
285ml (½ pint) red grape concentrate
2 dsp port essence
Invert sugar as required

1 Cut the washed, dried bananas into small pieces, put in saucepan with 1.7 litres/3 pts water, boil, and simmer for 25 minutes.

2 Strain into bucket add sugar and stir till dissolved.

3 Wash the fresh fruit; liquidise or mash it. Add to bucket with 1 litre/2 pts warm water and a Campden tablet; cover.

4 After 24 hours add liquidised/mashed bilberries. Make up to 4 litres/7 pts with warm water.

5 When 21°C/70°F add acid, pectic enzyme, nutrient salts, vitamin tablet and yeast starter.

6 Cover, ferment for 3 days, stirring twice daily.

7 Strain into a second bucket, discarding solids. Add grape concentrate.

8 Ferment for 2 days. Transfer to a demijohn under airlock.

9 Add port essence. Top up at end of heavy ferment. Each time s.g. drops to 1006 add 142ml/¼pt invert sugar.

10 At end of the ferment, rack, add 1 Campden tablet and sweeten to 1026.

11 Rack again after 28 days and again 2 months later.

To be at its best, keep for at least 12 months, adding a small amount of brandy to taste.

POTATO

(A SWEET SOCIAL WINE)

Sauternes or all-purpose yeast starter
2.3kg (5 lb) old potatoes
1.6kg (3½ lb) granulated sugar
1 heaped tsp citric acid
3 3mg vitamin B1 tablets
1 level tsp tartaric acid
1 level tsp grape tannin
1 level tsp pectic enzyme
1 level tsp nutrient salts
227ml (8 fl oz) white grape concentrate
Campden tablet as per instructions

1 Peel and wash the potatoes well and cut them into pieces.

2 Boil in 2 litres (4 pints) of water until they are soft (but not mashed).

3 Place the sugar in a sterilised bucket and strain the potato water over it, taking note of the quantity of water.

4 Stir until the sugar has dissolved, and make it up to 4.2 litres (7½ pints) with cold water.

5 When the temperature is down to 21°C (70°F) add the remaining ingredients except the grape concentrate, and ferment in the bucket for 4 days, stirring daily.

6 Transfer to a demijohn under airlock, adding the grape concentrate and topping up as necessary.

7 Ferment to a finish in a warm place, racking as soon as the wine is stable and adding 1 Campden tablet.

This wine is slow-maturing so if possible leave in bulk for at least 12 months before sweetening to taste and bottling.

RAISIN
(A SWEET DESSERT WINE)

Sherry or Madeira yeast starter
1.4kg (3 lb) raisins
450g (1 lb) granulated sugar
Campden tablets as per instructions
1 heaped tsp citric acid
1 3mg vitamin B1 tablet
1 level tsp pectic enzyme
1 level tsp nutrient salts

1 Wash the raisins thoroughly, chop or liquidise them in a little water. Place them in a sterilised bucket with the sugar.

2 Pour 2 litres (4 pints) of hot water over them, stirring them until the sugar has dissolved.

3 Make it up to 4.5 litres (8 pints) with cold water, add 1 Campden tablet and leave overnight, covered.

4 After 24 hours add the remaining ingredients, including the yeast starter, and ferment on the pulp for 5 days, stirring daily, before straining off the solids into a demijohn under airlock, topping up with cold water as necessary.

5 Ferment to a finish in a warm place, adding additional sugar in
   142ml (¼ pint) lots as the specific gravity drops to 1006.

6 Rack as soon as the wine is stable, adding 1 Campden tablet,
   and rack a second time after a further 4 weeks.

7 Mature in a cool place in the demijohn as long as possible as this
   will greatly improve the wine. It could be drunk after 4–6
   months.

REDCURRANT
(A ROSÉ TABLE WINE)

Champagne yeast starter
900g (2 lb) redcurrants
114g (4 oz) raspberries
Campden tablet as per instructions
1020g (2¼ lb) granulated sugar
227ml (8 fl oz) white grape concentrate
1 level tsp pectic enzyme
1 level tsp nutrient salts

1 Remove the stems from the redcurrants and raspberries and wash them well.

2 Liquidise the fruit in 1.7 litres (3 pints) of water or mash it.

3 Place it in a sterilised bucket. Add 1 Campden tablet, cover, and leave overnight.

4 The next day strain off the solids, dissolve the sugar in 1.7 litres (3 pints) of hot water and add this to the bucket, together with the grape concentrate.

5 Make it up to 4.5 litres (8 pints) with cold water, and when the temperature is down to 21°C (70°F) add the remaining ingredients, including the yeast starter.

6   Cover, and ferment in the bucket for 5 days before transferring to a demijohn under airlock.

7   Ferment to a finish in a warm place, racking as soon as the wine is stable.

This is a light wine and may be drunk young.

REVERENDINE
(A DELICIOUS GOLDEN LIQUEUR)

A golden wine
Reverendine essence
Caster sugar to taste
Glycerin
Vodka or Polish spirit
Tartaric acid

Note that the quantities of the ingredients are not shown – this is deliberate, for so much depends on the wine selected. It should be as strong in alcohol as possible (in order to keep down the cost of vodka) but should not have a strong flavour.

1   Take an empty sterilised bottle and pour in about 390ml (13 fl oz) of the wine.

2   Add 2 tsp of Reverendine essence and shake until it is well blended. Taste to ensure that the original wine flavour has been completely overcome and the herb flavour is correct, if not add a further small quantity of the essence.

3   Add caster sugar (again the quantity depends entirely on the sweetness of the wine base).

4   Shake thoroughly until all the sugar has dissolved – taste for sweetness.

5 Add about 1½ tsp of glycerin to add body, and finally the vodka or Polish spirit to gain an alcoholic content of about 56 proof. Here you will need to use the Pearson Square (see page 31) to assess the quantity.

6 Again taste, for it is likely that in blending and sweetening, the liqueur may need the addition of a pinch or two of tartaric acid to balance it.

7 Shake the bottle well to assist in blending; it may be drunk at once, but obviously improves greatly if allowed to blend and mature naturally.

RHUBARB
(A LIGHT, DRY TABLE WINE)

Champagne yeast starter
1.8kg (4 lb) rhubarb
900g (2 lb) granulated sugar
2 pints (1 litre) grape juice
  (N.B. containing no preservatives)
1 3mg vitamin B1 tablet
½ level tsp grape tannin
1 level tsp pectic enzyme
1 level tsp nutrient salts

Probably as it is grown in many gardens, beginners' first thoughts often turn to rhubarb wine. This is perhaps unfortunate, for although rhubarb does make a fine wine, it does have rather particular difficulties. It contains an unwanted acid known as oxalic acid in globules in the sticks, which occasionally causes destruction of the yeast. For this reason it has to have special treatment.

1 Wash the rhubarb well, slice it longways and then cut into 2 in (5cm) lengths.

2 Place it in a bucket, add 3.7 litres (6½ pts) of cold water (this avoids the extraction of the oxalic acid), then add all the ingredients and the yeast starter, cover, and keep in a warm place.

3 Ferment for 2 days, stirring daily, then strain into a second bucket.

4 Transfer to a demijohn under airlock as soon as this ferment is complete (4–5 days).

5 Ferment to a finish in a warm place, rack as usual, but store in a jar under airlock as this wine does sometimes have what is known as a 'malolactic ferment'. This, which is rather like a secondary ferment, occurs when ingredients containing large amounts of malic acid (such as rhubarb) are used.

The wine may be drunk after 4 months.

RICE & RAISIN

(A MEDIUM-SWEET SOCIAL WINE)

All-purpose yeast starter
800g (13/4 lb) rice (short pudding rice)
450g (1 lb) raisins
1.1kg (2½ lb) granulated sugar
2 oranges
Campden tablets as per instructions
1 3mg vitamin B1 tablet
2 level tsp citric acid
1 level tsp pectic enzyme
1 level tsp nutrient salts

1   Wash the rice and raisins. Chop the raisins and place them in a sterilised bucket.

2   Add the sugar, rice, juice and thinly peeled skins of the oranges, being careful to avoid the pith.

3   Pour on 2 litres (4 pints) of boiling water, and stir until the sugar has dissolved. Then add 1 Campden tablet, cover, and leave overnight.

4   After 24 hours make it up to 4.5 litres (8 pints) with warm water, and when the temperature is down to 21°C (70°F) add the remaining ingredients, including the yeast starter.

5 Ferment on the pulp for 6 days, stirring daily, before straining the fermenting must into a demijohn under airlock.

6 Continue the fermentation to completion, and rack as soon as the wine is stable and add a Campden tablet.

This wine may be drunk very young if fined or filtered, but if it is to be kept, add 1 Campden tablet and store for about 9 months.

ROSE HIP SYRUP

(A LIGHT, MEDIUM-SWEET TABLE WINE)

Bordeaux or all-purpose yeast starter
1020g (2¼ lb) granulated sugar
340ml (12 fl oz) rose hip syrup
2 3mg vitamin B1 tablets
1 heaped tsp citric acid
1 level tsp pectic enzyme
1 level tsp nutrient salts
Campden tablet as per instructions

1 Place the sugar in a sterilised bucket, add 2 pints (1 litre) of hot water and stir well until the sugar has dissolved.

2 Make it up to 4.2 litres (7½ pints) with cold water, and when the temperature is down to 21°C (70°F) add the remaining ingredients, including the yeast starter.

3 Cover, and ferment in the bucket for 4 days, stirring daily, before transferring to a demijohn under airlock.

4 Ferment to a finish in a warm place, racking as soon as the wine is stable, at which stage a Campden tablet should be added.

This wine is a general purpose wine, but a pleasant one, and very easy to make. If it goes to dryness it may be sweetened to taste after the maturation period. It could be drunk after 4 months.

ROSE PETAL
(A LIGHT, FRAGRANT ROSÉ TABLE WINE)

Bordeaux or all-purpose yeast starter
2 litres (4 pints) rose petals (loosely packed)
900g (2 lb) granulated sugar
114g (4 oz) raspberries
114g (4 oz) redcurrants
Campden tablet as per instructions
285ml (½ pint) white grape concentrate
2 3mg vitamin B1 tablets
1 level tsp citric acid
1 level tsp tartaric acid
1 level tsp nutrient salts
1 level tsp pectic enzyme
1 level tsp grape tannin

1 Take the rose petals, which can be a blend of colours, though a few should be dark red, rinse them lightly and place them in a sterilised bucket, together with the sugar.

2 Add 2 litres (4 pints) of tepid water, and stir until the sugar has dissolved.

3 Wash the fruit and liquidise it in a little water (or mash it). Place it in the bucket, together with 1 Campden tablet.

4 Cover, and leave for 24 hours.

5 Add the grape concentrate and the remaining ingredients, including the yeast starter, and make it up to 4.5 litres (8 pints) by adding cold water.

6 Ferment on the pulp for 4 days, stirring daily, before straining off the solids and putting the fermenting must into a demijohn under airlock.

7 Ferment to a finish in a warm place, racking as soon as the wine is stable.

This wine does not need a long maturation period, and may be drunk as a light, fresh wine within 4 or 5 months.

SLOE

(A MEDIUM-SWEET SOCIAL WINE)

Burgundy or all-purpose yeast starter
1.4kg (3 lb) sloes (with stalks removed)
227g (½ lb) sultanas
1.4kg (3 lb) granulated sugar
Campden tablets as per instructions
1 3mg vitamin B1 tablet
1 level tsp pectic enzyme
1 level tsp nutrient salts

1 Wash the sloes thoroughly. Cut or prick them and place them in a sterilised bucket.

2 Wash the sultanas. Liquidise them in a little water or chop them.

3 Add them to the bucket with the sugar. Pour in 2 litres (4 pints) of boiling water. Stir until the sugar has dissolved, add 1 Campden tablet, cover, and leave overnight.

4 After 24 hours, make it up to 4.5 litres (8 pints) with warm water, and when the temperature is down to 21°C (70°F) add the remaining ingredients, including the yeast starter.

5 Ferment on the pulp for 4 days, stirring daily, before straining the fermenting must into a demijohn under airlock and topping up if necessary.

6 Continue the fermentation to completion in a warm place, racking as soon as the wine is stable, and adding 1 Campden tablet.

This wine could be drunk after 6 months but will improve greatly with keeping. Sweeten to taste a few days before bottling.

SULTANA

(A MEDIUM, WHITE TABLE WINE)

Hock or all-purpose yeast starter
900g (2 lb) bananas
900g (2 lb) granulated sugar
900g (2 lb) sultanas
1 level tsp pectic enzyme
Campden tablets as per instructions
2 level tsp citric acid
1 level tsp nutrient salts
2 3mg vitamin B1 tablets

1 Peel the bananas, discard their skins and chop them up.

2 Simmer them in 1.7 litres (3 pints) of water for 30 minutes. Strain, and place the liquor and the sugar into a sterilised bucket, stirring until the sugar has dissolved.

3 Thoroughly wash the sultanas. Liquidise them in a little water or chop them.

4 Add them to the bucket. Make it up to 3.4 litres (6 pints) with cold water, and when the temperature is down to 21°C (70°F) add the pectic enzyme and a Campden tablet, cover, and leave overnight.

5 After 24 hours make it up to 4.5 litres (8 pints) with warm water and add the acid, nutrient salts, vitamin B1 tablets and the yeast starter.

6 Ferment on the pulp for 4 days, stirring daily, before straining the fermenting must into a demijohn under airlock, topping up as necessary with cold water.

7 Ferment to a finish in a warm place, racking immediately the wine is stable, and adding 1 Campden tablet. A second racking will be necessary within 4 weeks.

This wine could be drunk after 4 months.

TEA & RAISIN

(A MEDIUM-SWEET SOCIAL WINE)

Sherry or all-purpose yeast starter
4 tbsp tea leaves
900g (2 lb) granulated sugar
900g (2 lb) raisins
1 heaped tsp citric acid
1 level tsp pectic enzyme
1 level tsp nutrient salts

1 Select a scented Indian or China tea, and tie it in a muslin bag.

2 Place the bag in a sterilised bucket and pour 2 litres (4 pints) of boiling water over it.

3 Add the sugar and stir until it has all dissolved.

4 Wash the raisins thoroughly in warm water. Liquidise or mash them in 1.7 litres (3 pints) of warm water. Add this to the bucket.

5 Make it up to 4.5 litres (8 pints) with cold water, take out the bag of tea, and when the temperature is down to 21°C (70°F) add the remaining ingredients, including the yeast starter.

6 Ferment for 5 days before straining into a demijohn under airlock.

7 Ferment to a finish in a warm place, racking as soon as the wine is stable.

8 Sweeten to taste, adding one stabilising tablet.

The wine could be drunk after 3–4 months.

VERMOUTH
(A SWEET APERITIF)

This is an adaptation of the Grapefruit Aperitif recipe (see page 102), and we start with that finished wine. To this must be added the herbs, and the wine should be fortified to 30 proof spirit. The quantity of spirit required will depend on the strength of the grapefruit wine, and to measure this accurately we must use the Pearson Square (see page 31). Assuming that the wine is 26 proof and the spirit is 70 proof, then the ratio is 10 parts of wine to 1 part of spirit.

1 Buy a packet of Vermouth herbs suitable for a sweet aperitif, and make a small cotton bag, into which the herbs can be placed. Use the quantity of herbs recommended on the packet.

2 Tie a piece of cotton to the bag, and hang it in the demijohn (remembering to leave the cotton end outside the container) for 7–10 days (or until sufficient flavour has been extracted).

3 Move the bag about, and shake the container daily.

4 Remove the bag then add the spirit to the wine, shake well, and leave for a few days to allow a complete blending.

5 Sweeten to taste a few days before bottling.

This aperitif may be drunk after 4–5 months.

VINE PRUNINGS

(A LIGHT, DRY TABLE WINE)

Chablis or all-purpose yeast starter
2.3kg (5 lb) vine leaves and tendrils
Campden tablet as per instructions
1.4kg (3 lb) granulated sugar
1 3mg vitamin B1 tablet
1 heaped tsp citric acid
1 level tsp nutrient salts

1 Place the leaves and tendrils in a sterilised bucket and pour in 7 pints (4 litres) of boiling water and add a Campden tablet.

2 Let is stand for 48 hours, closely covered, but turn the leaves occasionally so that they are all submerged.

3 Strain the liquid into a second bucket containing the sugar.

4 Wash the leaves and tendrils in ½ litre (1 pint) of hot water, discard the leaves and tendrils and add the water to the bucket containing the sugar, and stir until the sugar has dissolved.

5 The remaining ingredients, including the yeast starter should then be added.

6 Ferment for 4 days before transferring to a demijohn under airlock, and continue the fermentation to completion in a warm place, racking as soon as the wine is stable. A second racking is advisable after a further 28 days.

The wine could be drunk after 4 months.

WHEAT & RAISIN
(A MEDIUM-BODIED, SWEET SOCIAL WINE)

Sherry or all-purpose yeast starter
1 pint (½ litre) wheat
2 large potatoes
900g (2 lb) raisins
1.1kg (2½ lb) granulated sugar
2 level tsp citric acid
Campden tablets as per instructions
1 level tsp amylase
1 level tsp pectic enzyme
1 level tsp nutrient salts
1 3mg vitamin B1 tablet

1 Wash the wheat. Soak it overnight in ½ litre/1 pt of cold water to soften it.

2 Next day strain off and discard the liquid.

3 Wash (or peel if old) the potatoes and slice them.

4 Wash the raisins well in warm water. Liquidise them and the wheat in some water or chop the raisins and bruise the wheat. Place them in a bucket.

5 Add the sugar, potatoes, and acid, and pour over 1.7 litres /3 pts of hot (not boiling) water. Stir until the sugar has dissolved, and make it up to 4.5 litres/8 pts with cold water.

6 Add 1 Campden tablet. Cover and leave for 24 hours.

7 Add the amylase, pectic enzyme, nutrient salts, vitamin tablet and the yeast starter, stirring them in.

8 Ferment in a warrn place for 5 days, stirring at least once each day to break up the cap of solids which forms at the top of the fermenting must.

9 Strain off the solids, placing the fermenting must in a demijohn under airlock.

10 Ferment to a finish in a warm place. Rack as soon as the wine is stable and add 1 Campden tablet.

This wine may be drunk after 6–9 months but will improve greatly with keeping.

INDEX